The Contemporary Black Ink Drawings of Bobby J. Jones

Mr. Bobby J. Jones

DEDICATION

The Contemporary Black Ink Drawings of Bobby J. Jones. 2023.

Albuquerque Artist Bobby J. Jones created 30 plus contemporary black ink drawings for this coloring book publication. Jones became inspired after attending an art class at Mark Twain Elementary School with his student with special needs. Jones took the study course through study.com for Praxis Art Content Knowledge Exam. He learned about what the term contemporary means in art. One description focused upon art not being pretty. Jones views his black ink drawings as not being pretty. As a result, Bobby created this publication, The Contemporary Black Ink Drawings of Bobby J. Jones Coloring Book.

CONTENTS

THE CONTEMPORARY BLACK INK DRAWINGS OF BOBBY J. JONES

TRANSFORMATIONAL
HAGIOGRAPHY
EXPLAINS

CONTOUR LINES
ON
NEUTRAL SURFACES
TEMPT
EBONY LINES
MAKE BELIEVE
PORTRAITS
OF
RAMBLING
ART DRAWINGS
RAPTUROUSLY
YAMMERING

BOBBY'S NAME.
LOUDLY
ASTOUNDING
CREATIVITY
KEEPS

IMAGINATIVE
NUANCES
KNOWABLE

DOWNWARD
ROUNDING
AWESOME
WINDING
INK
NAMING
GEOMETRIC
SHAPES

OF
FABULOUS

BOUNDARIES
OFFERING
BEAUTIFUL
BORDERS
YEILDING

JUXTAPOSITIONAL

JUDICAL
OBDURATE
NURTURING
ENERGETIC
SHAPES.

BOBBY J. JONES
05/06/2023

Bobby J. Jones. Black Ink Drawing #1. 2023.

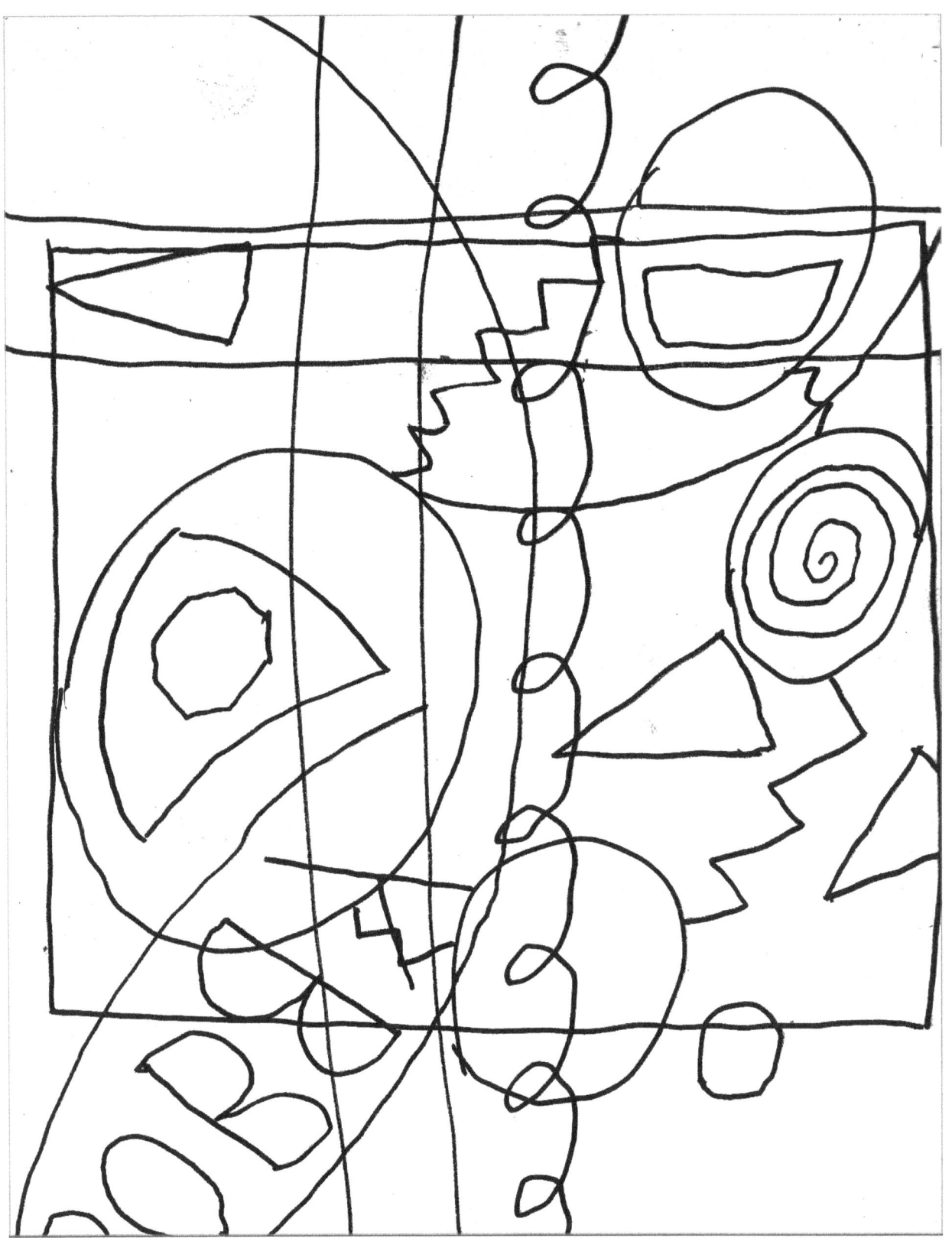

Bobby J. Jones. Black Ink Drawing #2. 2023.

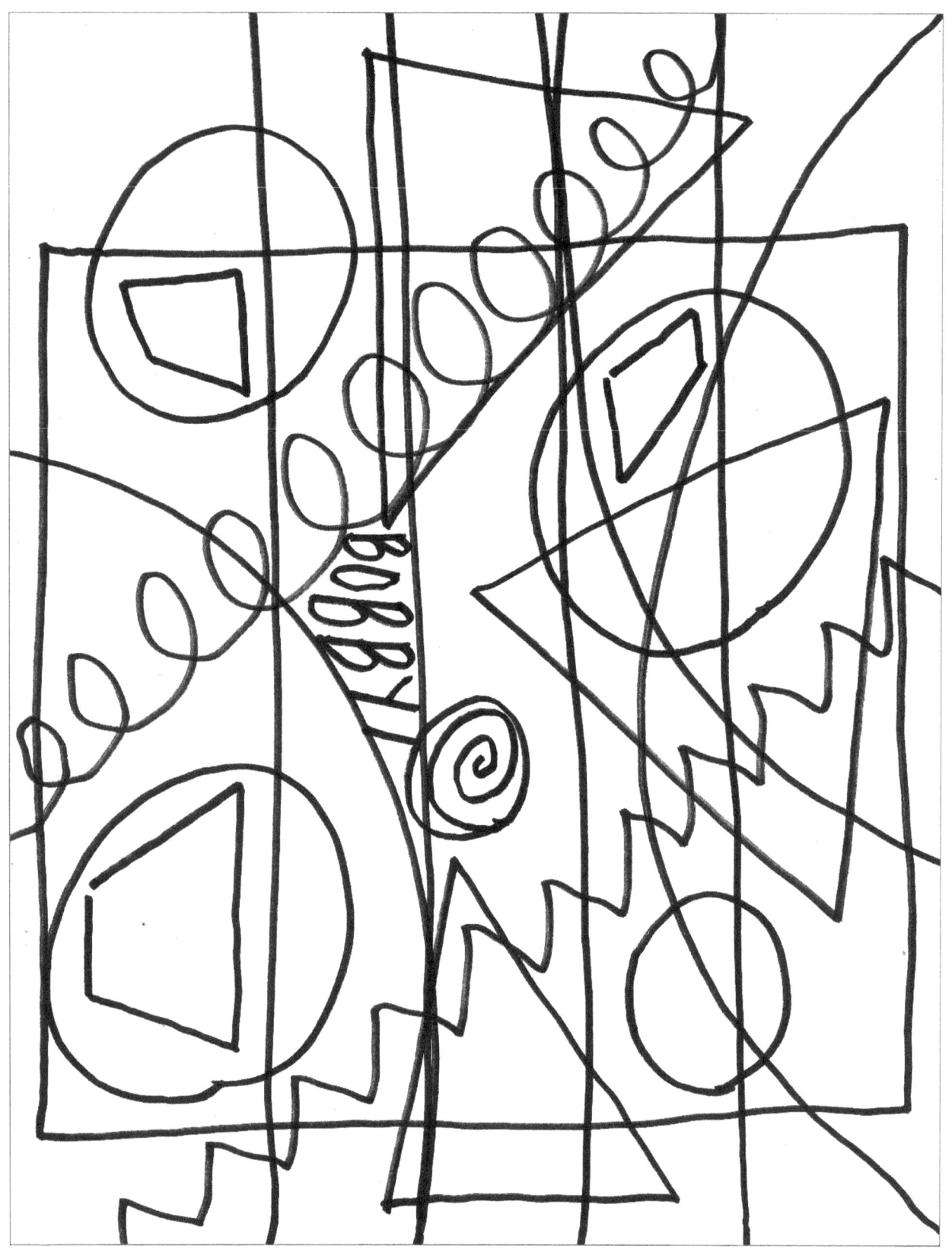

Bobby J. Jones. Black Ink Drawing #3. 2023.

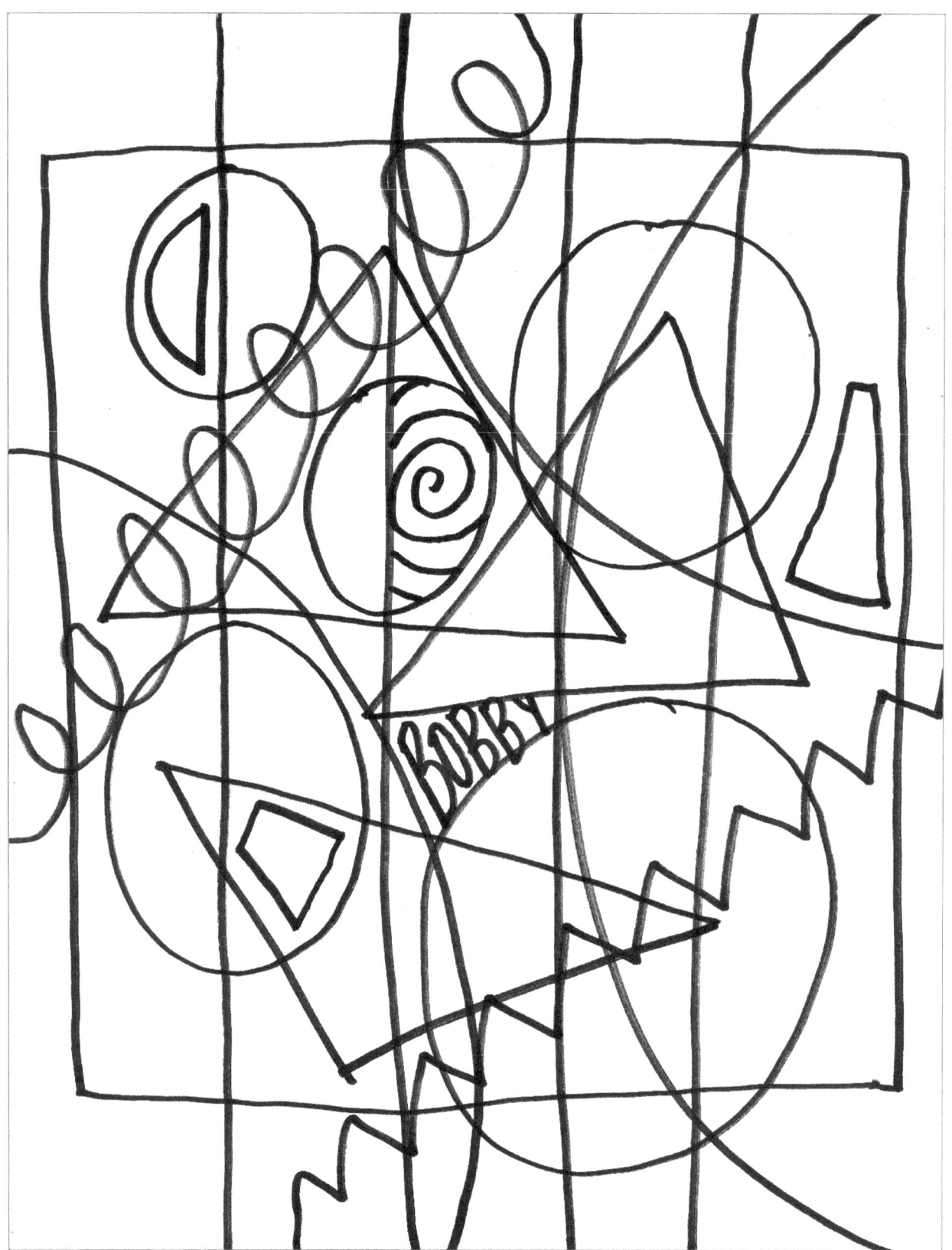

Bobby J. Jones. Black Ink Drawing #4. 2023.

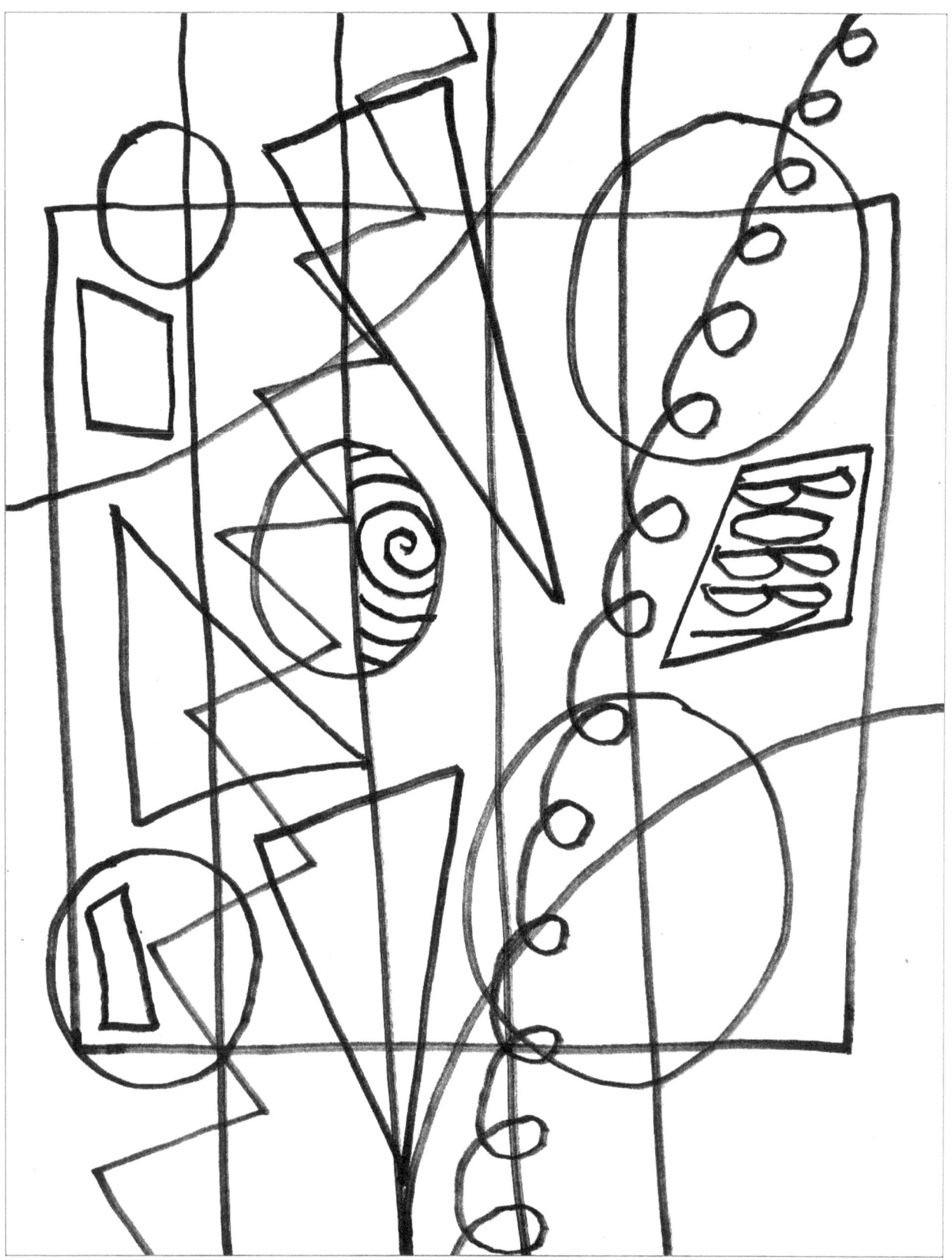

Bobby J. Jones. Black Ink Drawing #5. 2023.

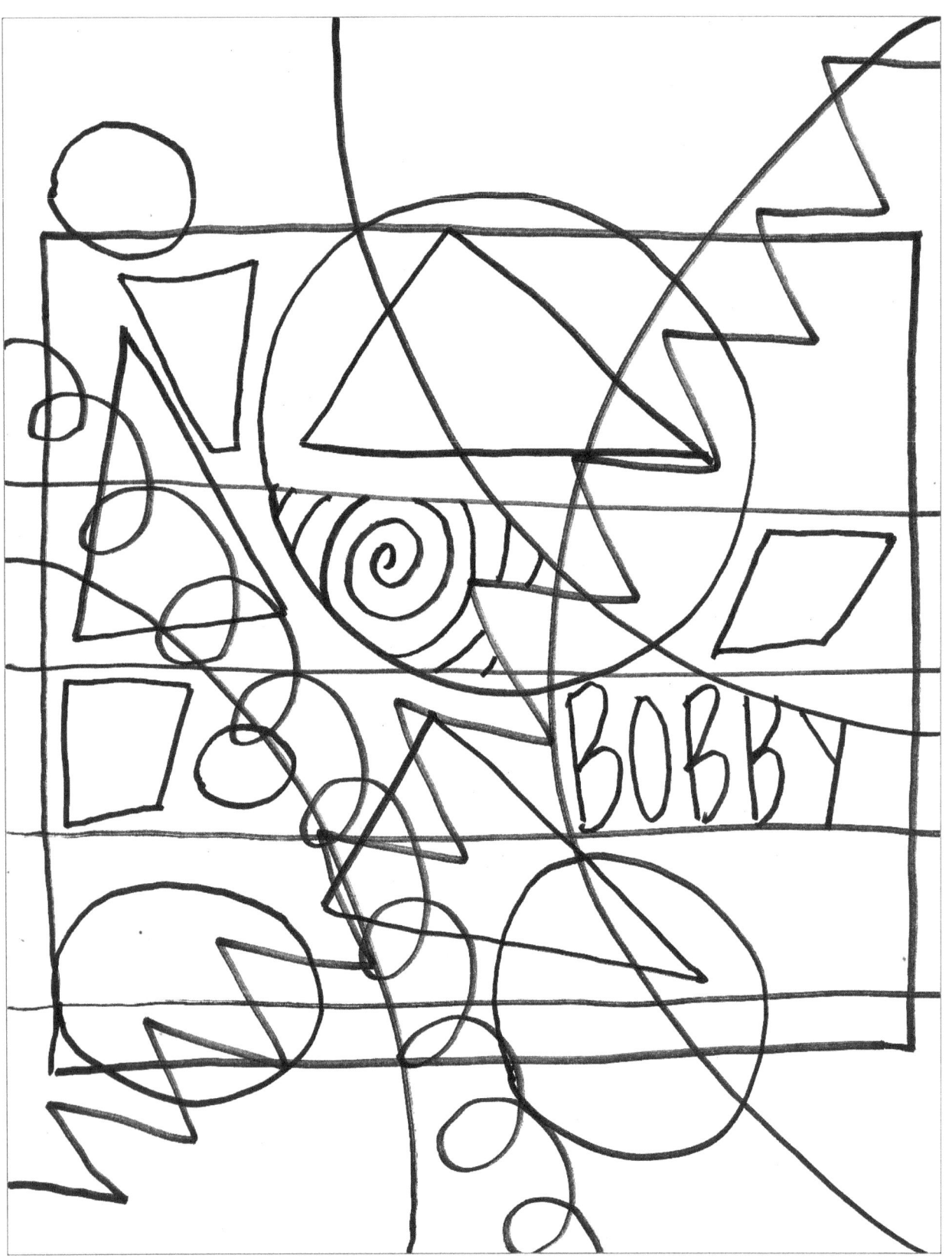

Bobby J. Jones. Black Ink Drawing #6. 2023.

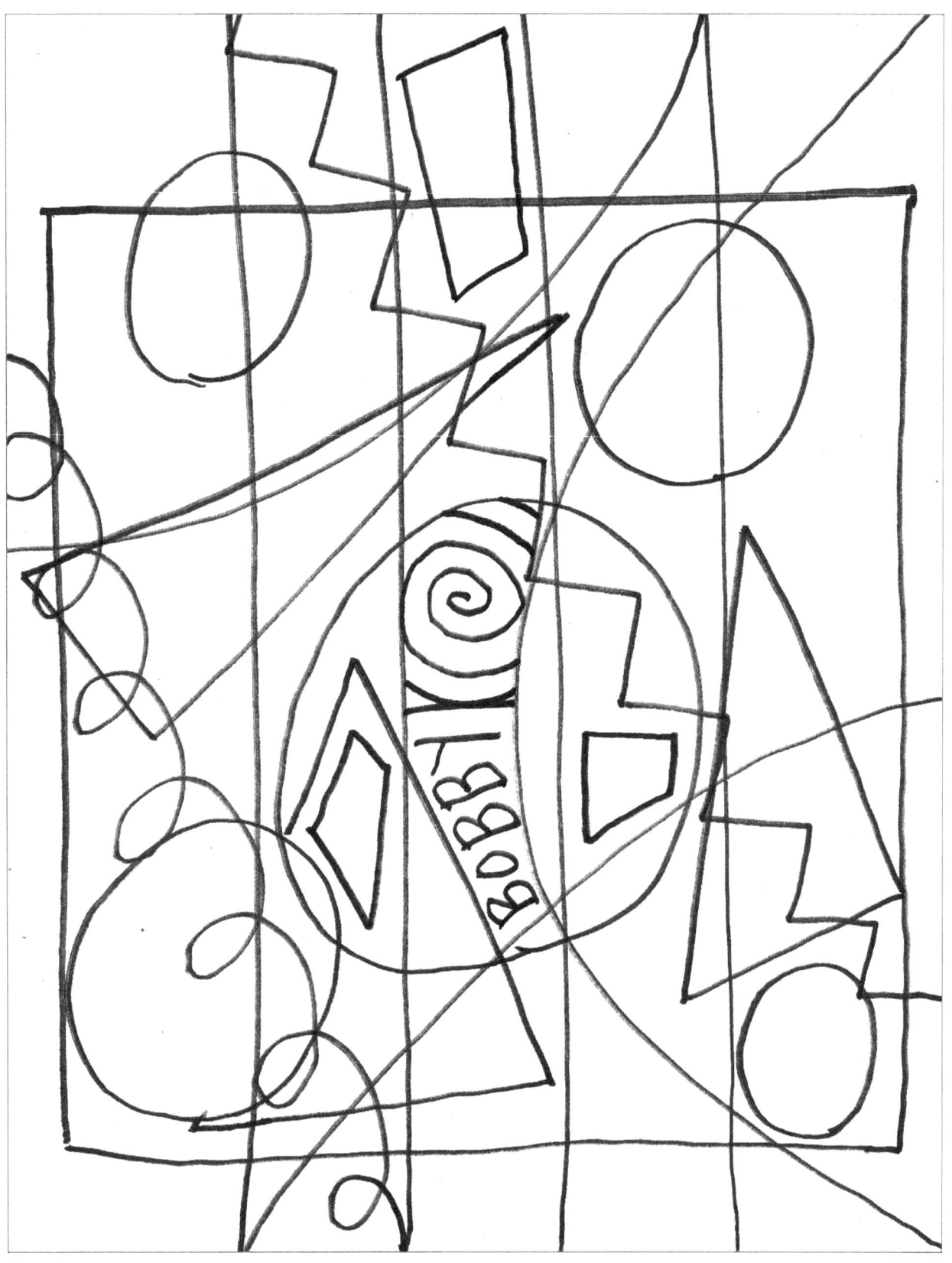

Bobby J. Jones. Black Ink Drawing #7. 2023.

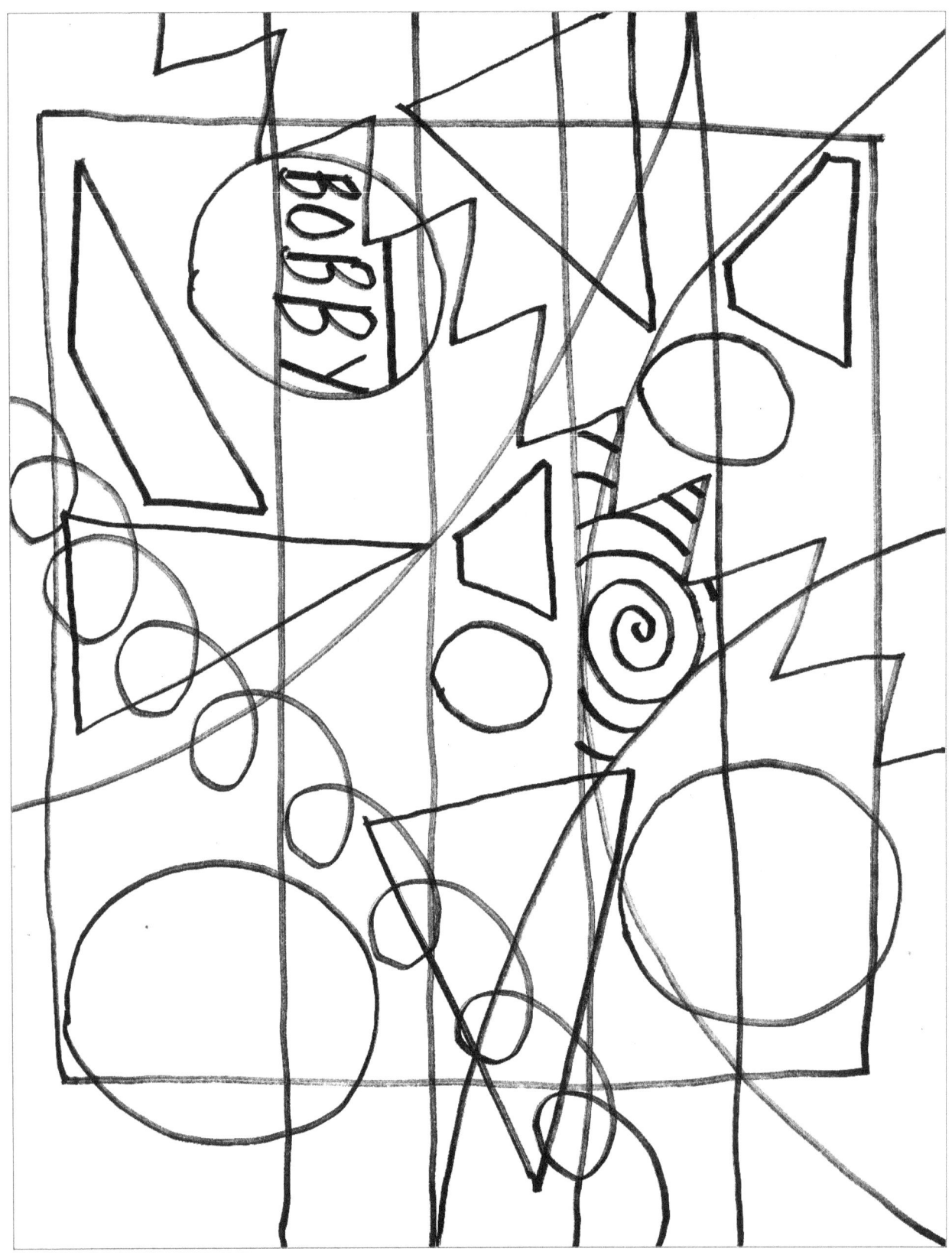

Bobby J. Jones. Black Ink Drawing #8. 2023.

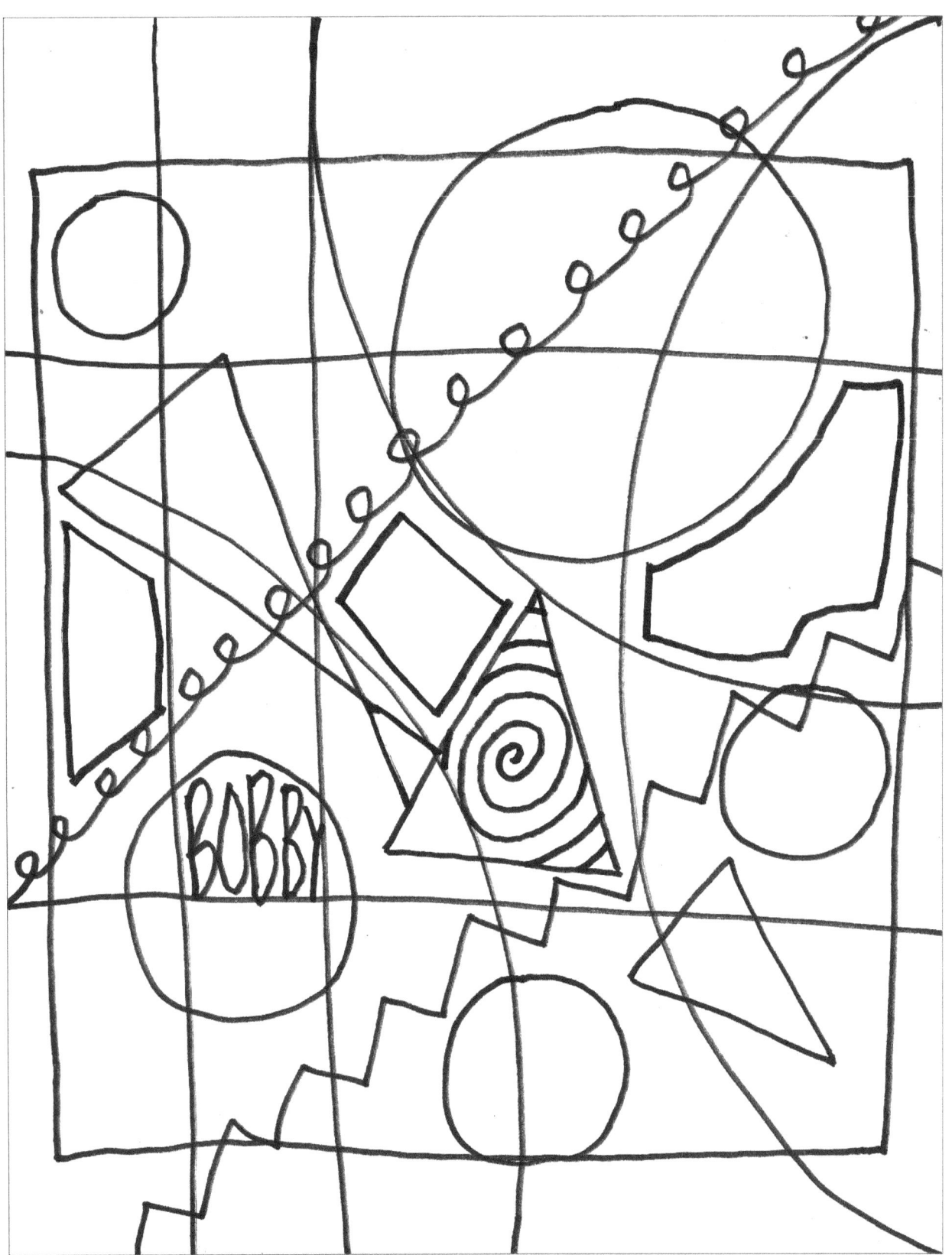

Bobby J. Jones. Black Ink Drawing #9. 2023.

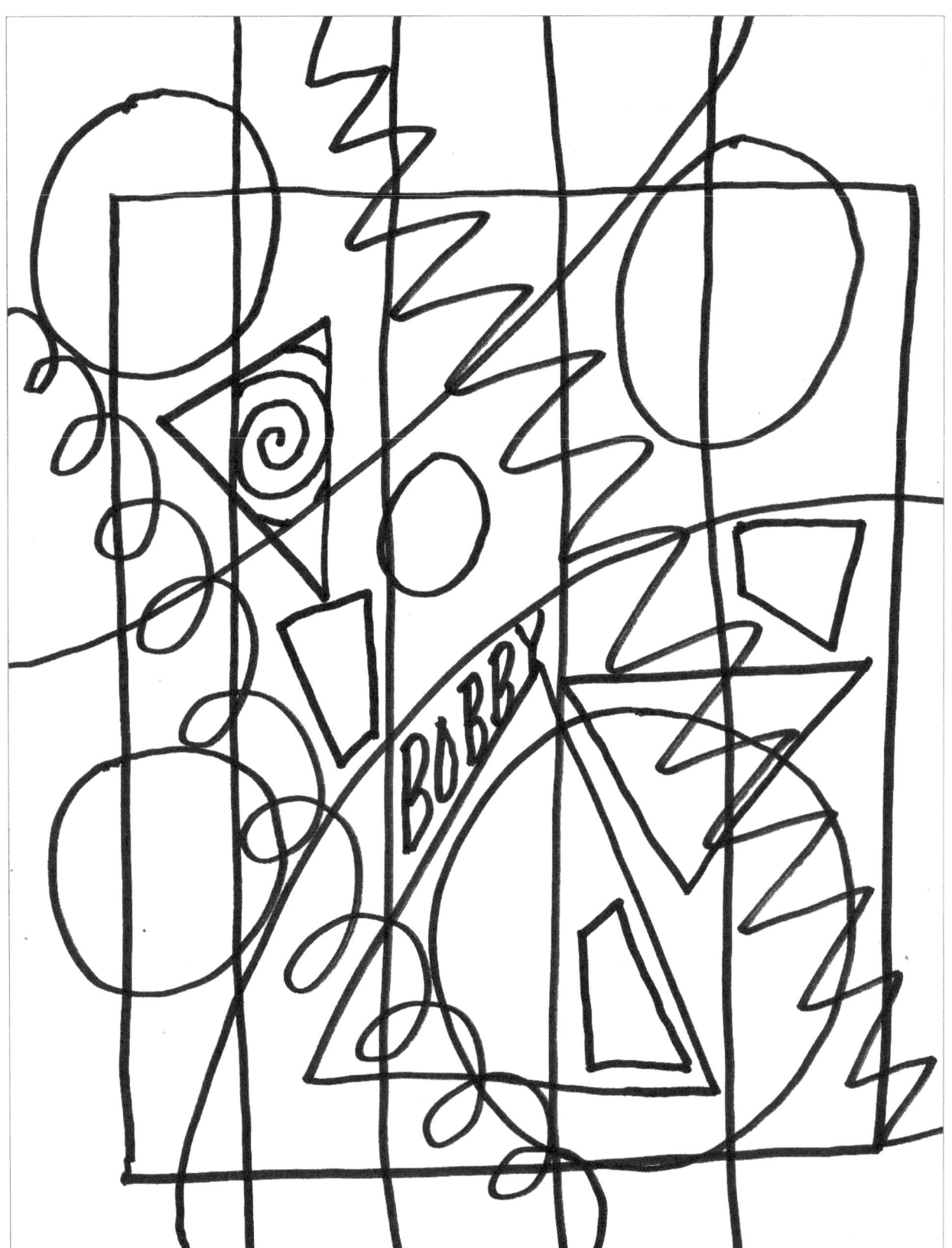

Bobby J. Jones. Black Ink Drawing #10. 2023.

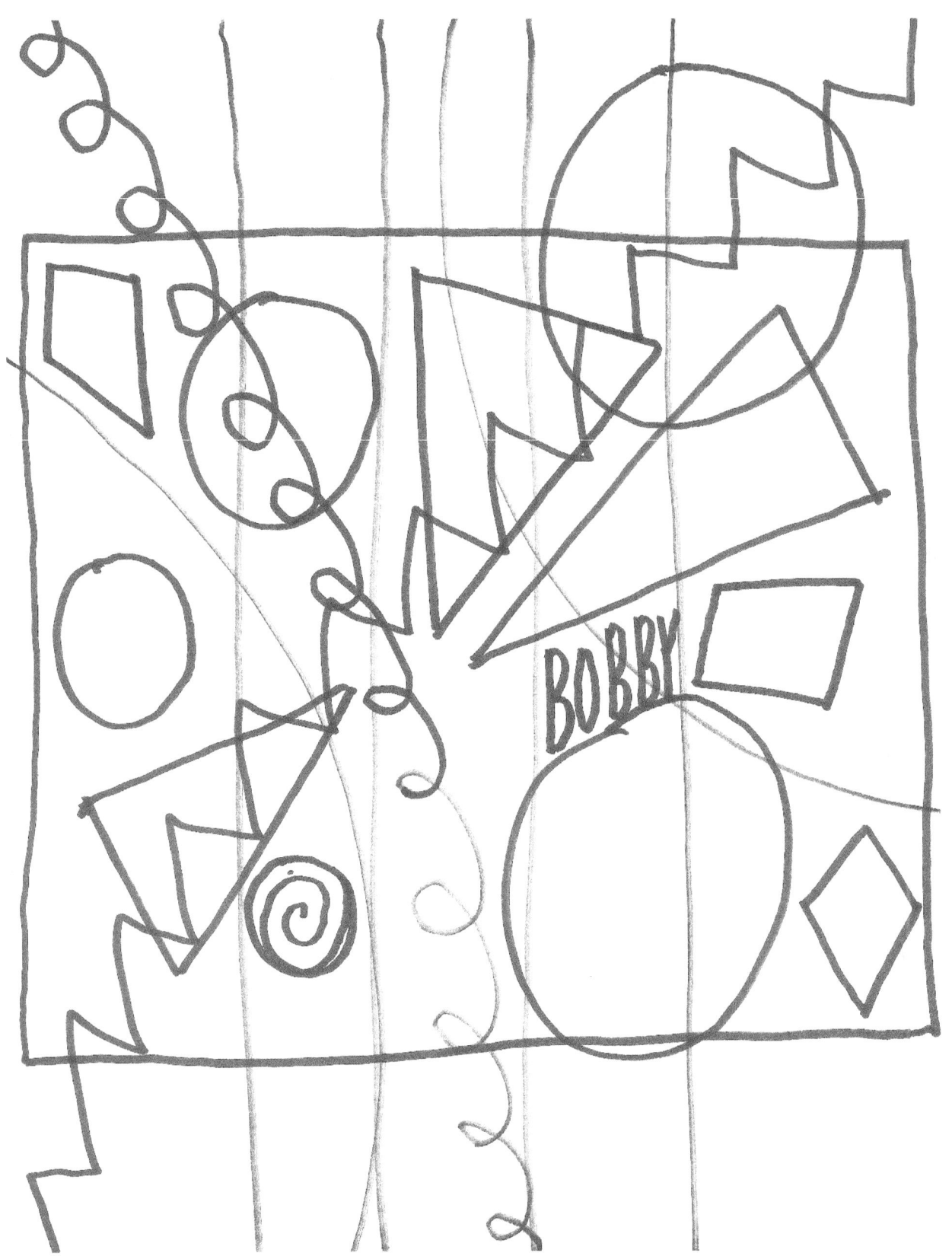

Bobby J. Jones. Black Ink Drawing #11. 2023.

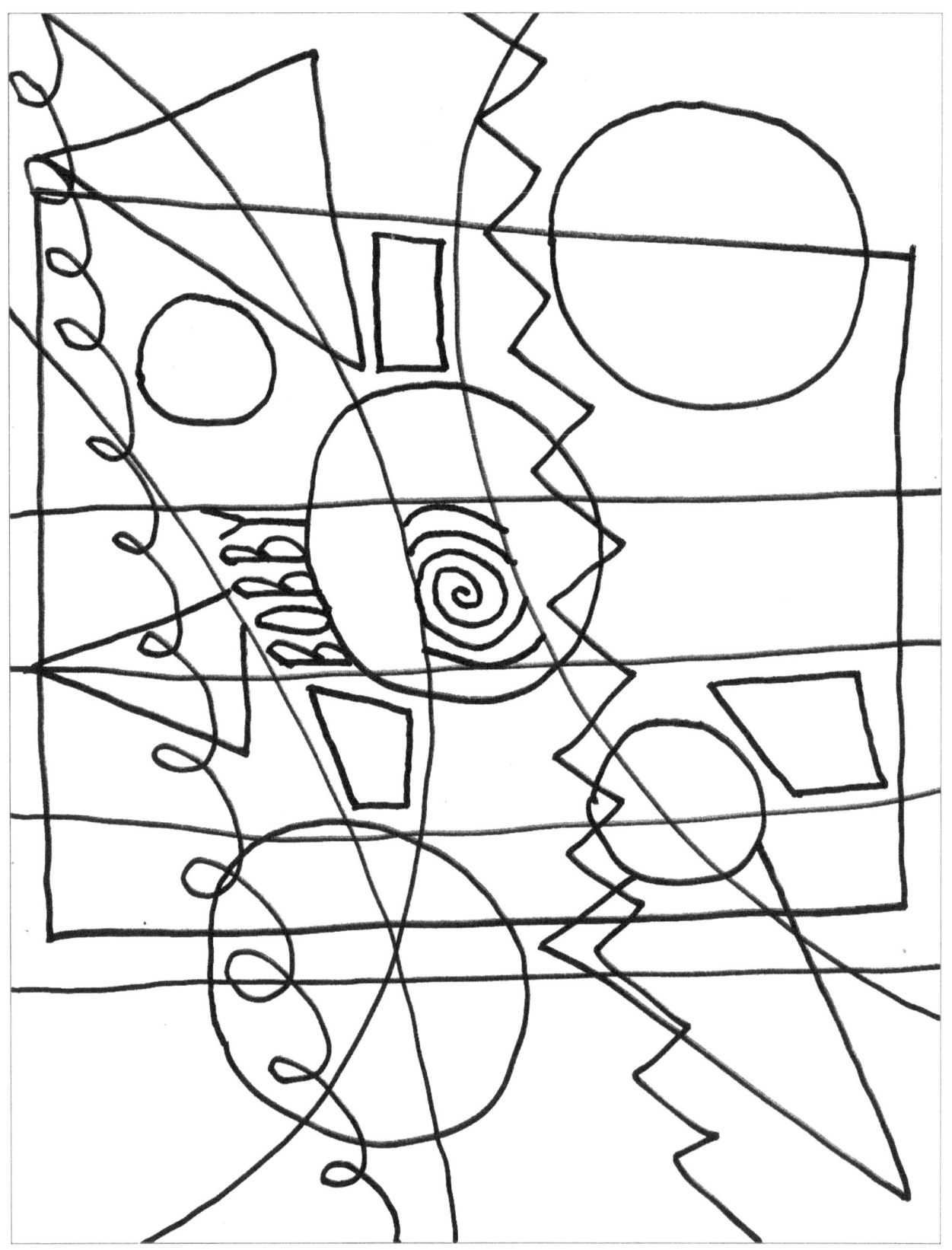

Bobby J. Jones. Black Ink Drawing #12. 2023.

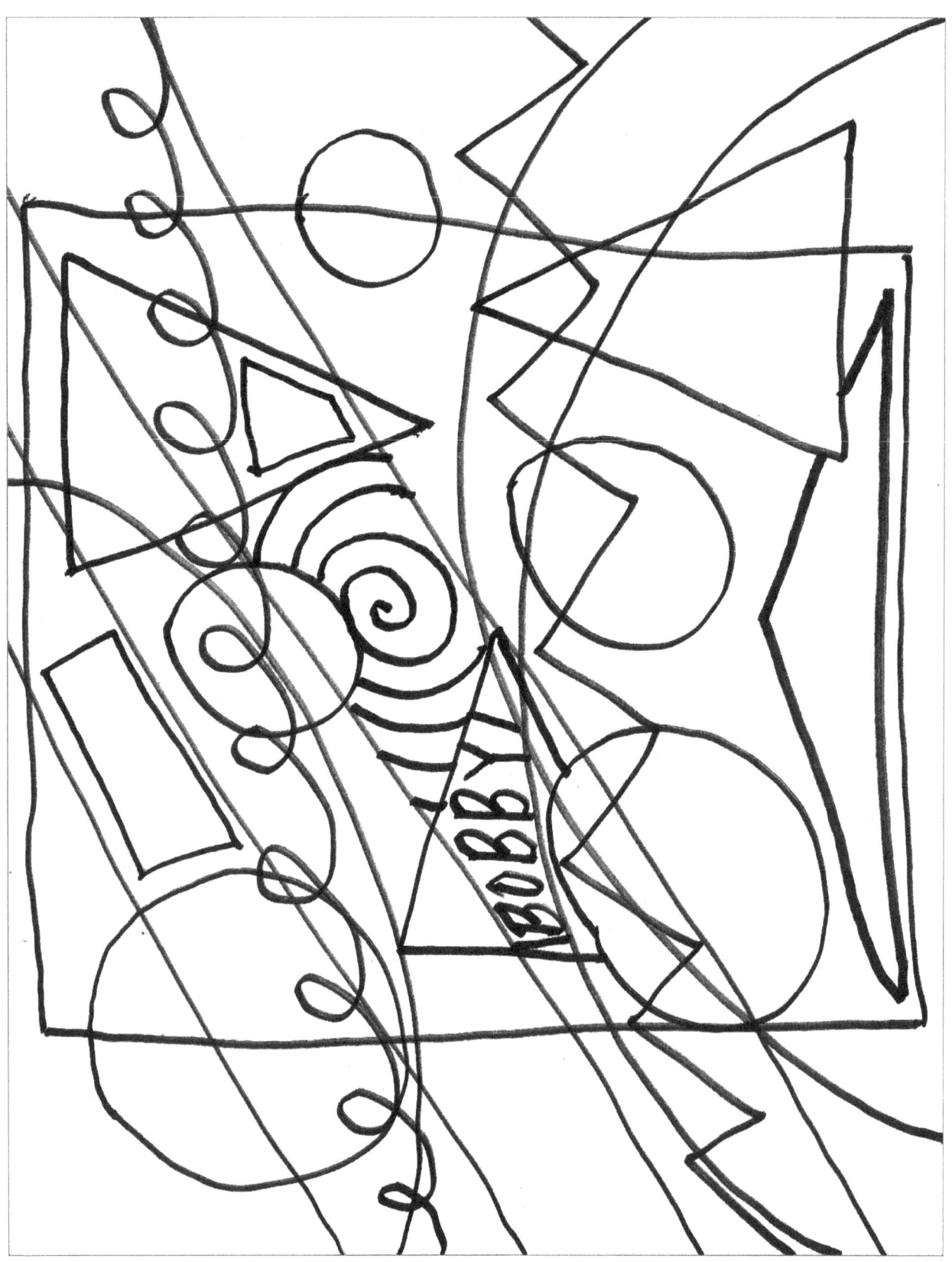

Bobby J. Jones. Black Ink Drawing #13. 2023.

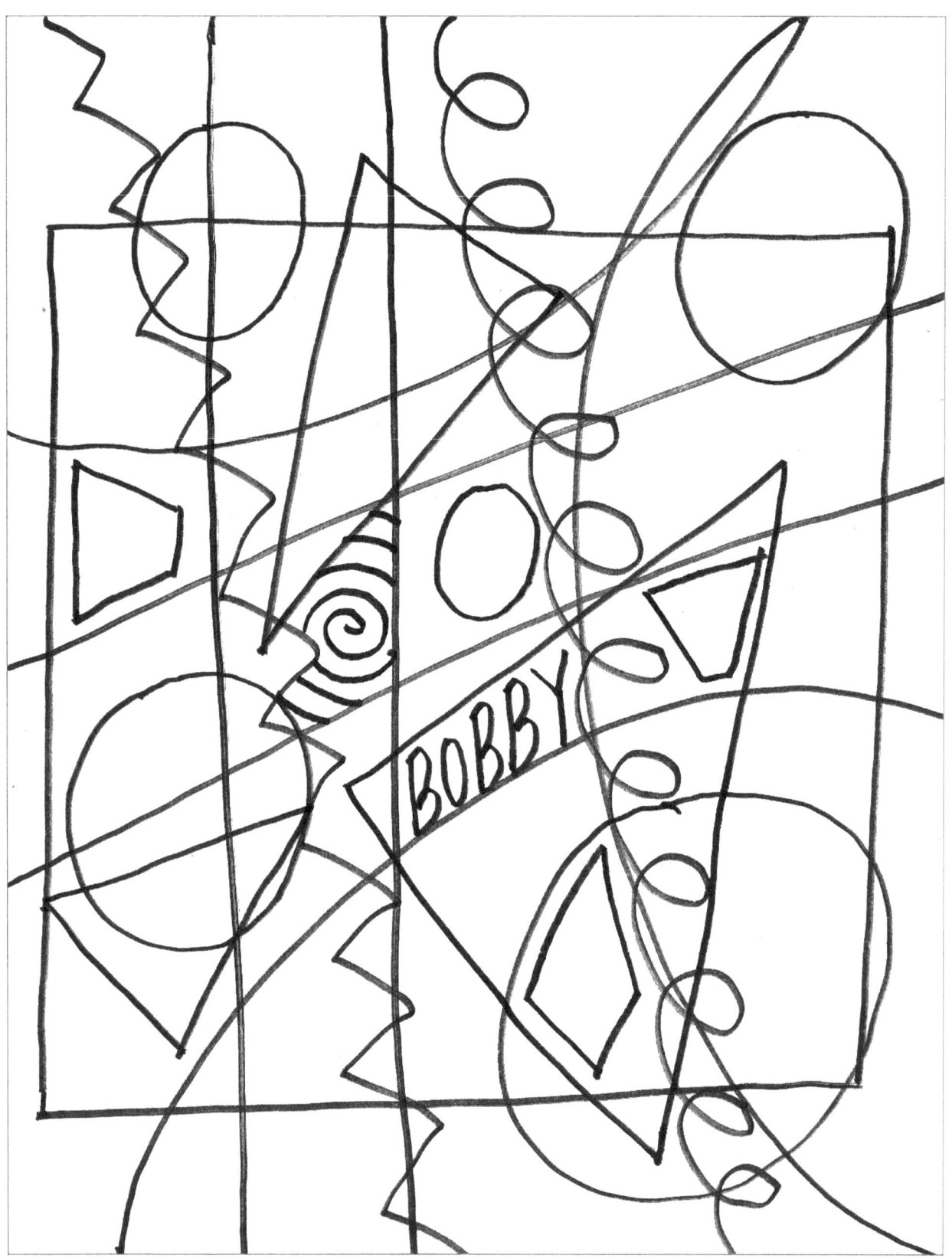

Bobby J. Jones. Black Ink Drawing #14. 2023.

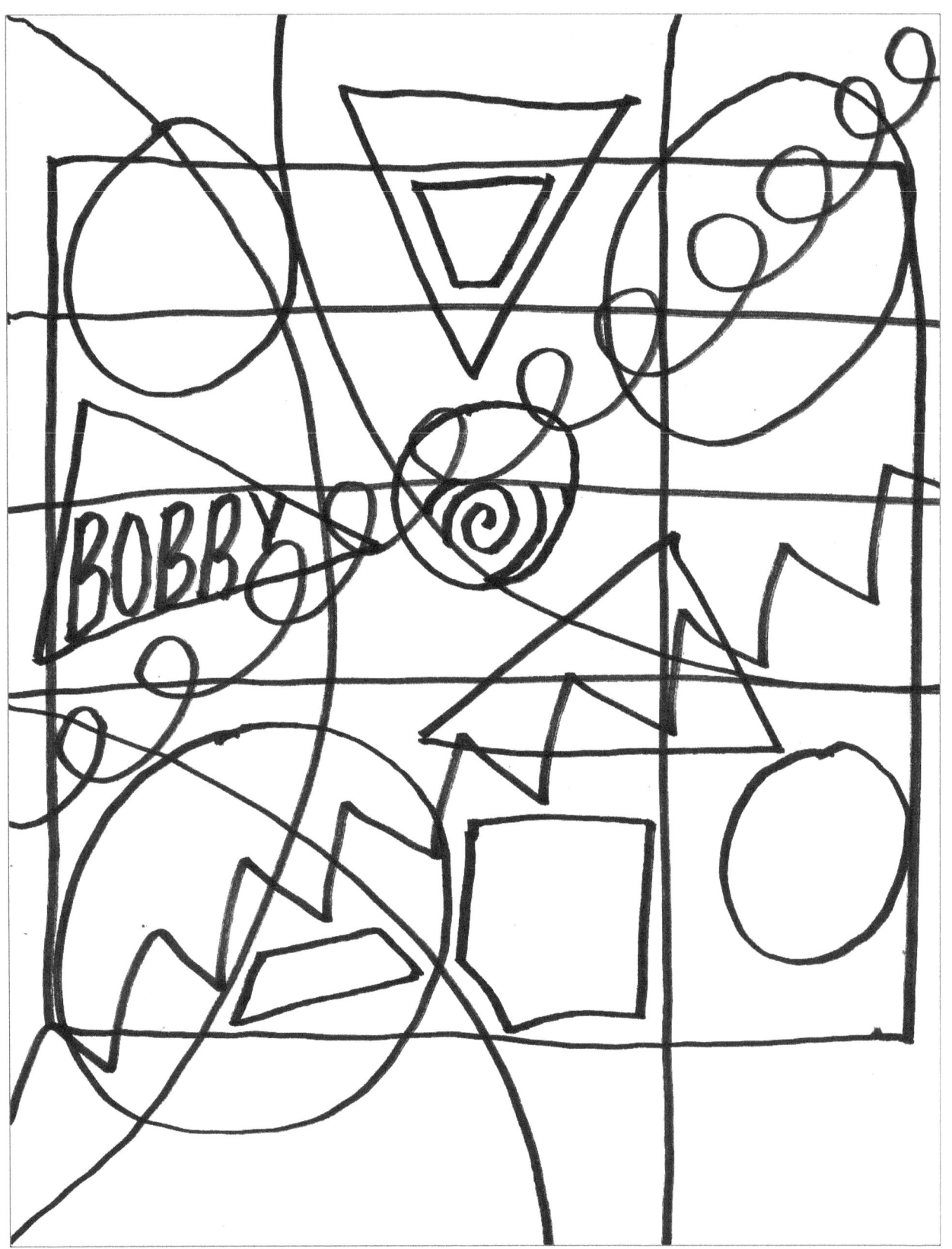

Bobby J. Jones. Black Ink Drawing #15. 2023.

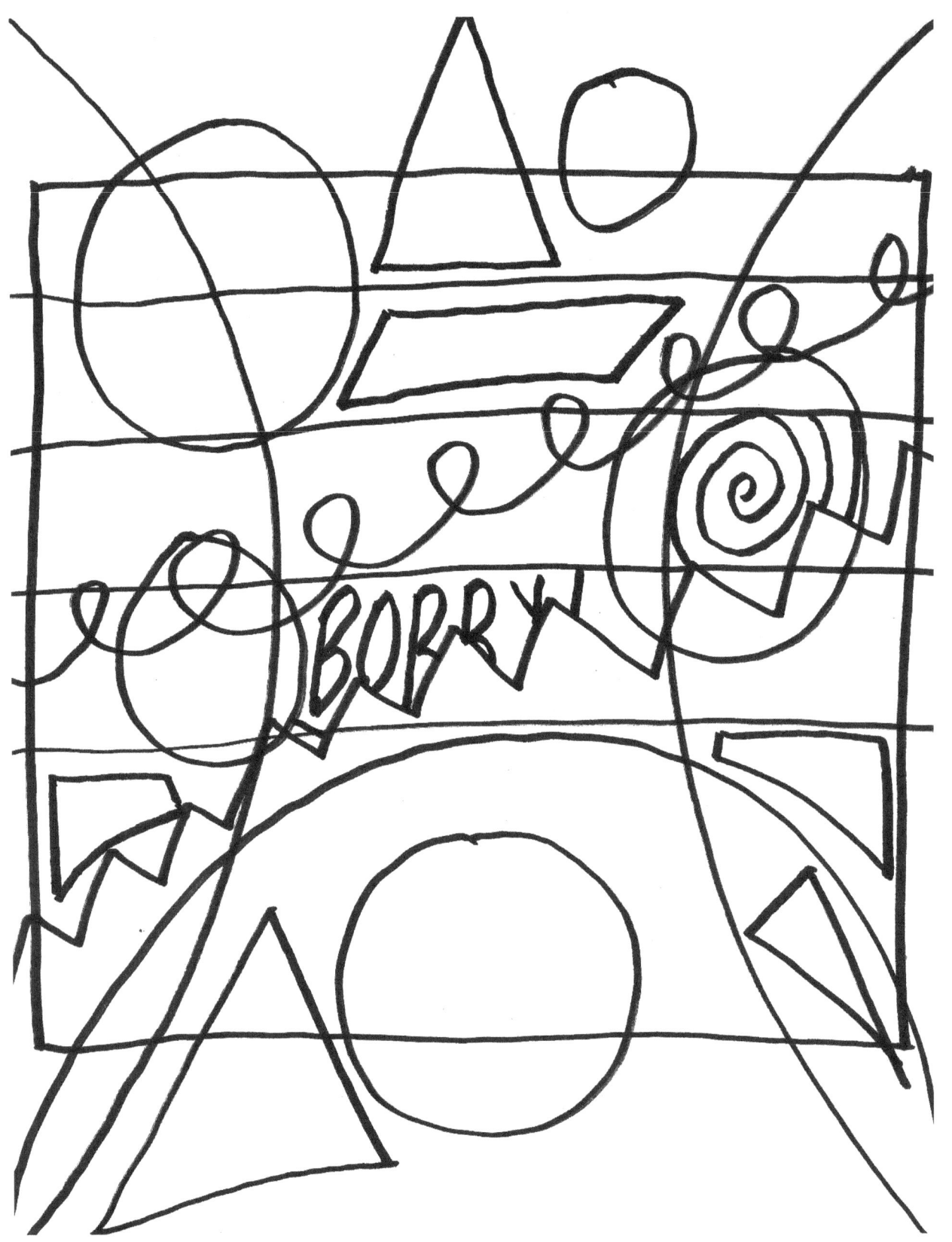

Bobby J. Jones. Black Ink Drawing #16. 2023.

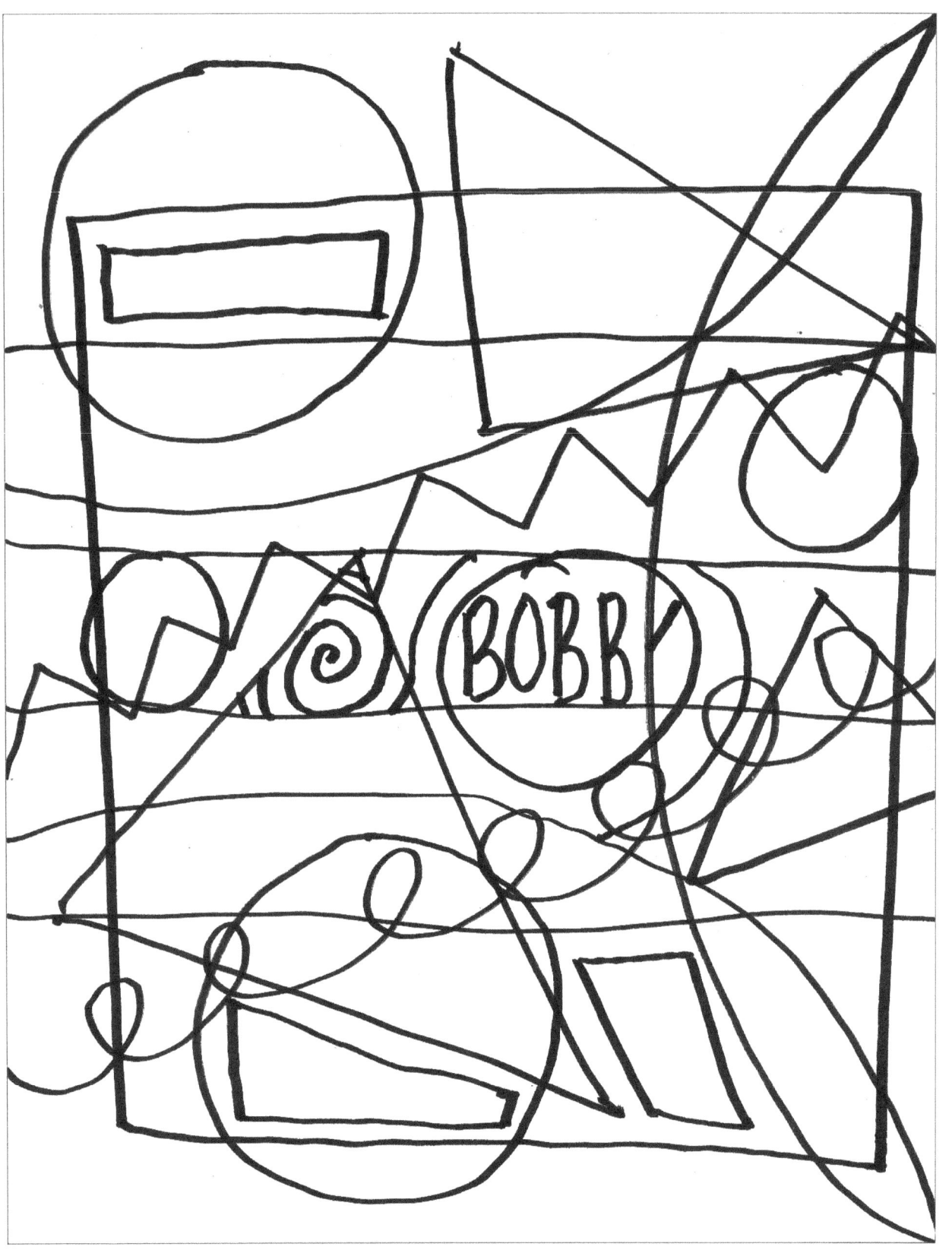

Bobby J. Jones. Black Ink Drawing #17. 2023.

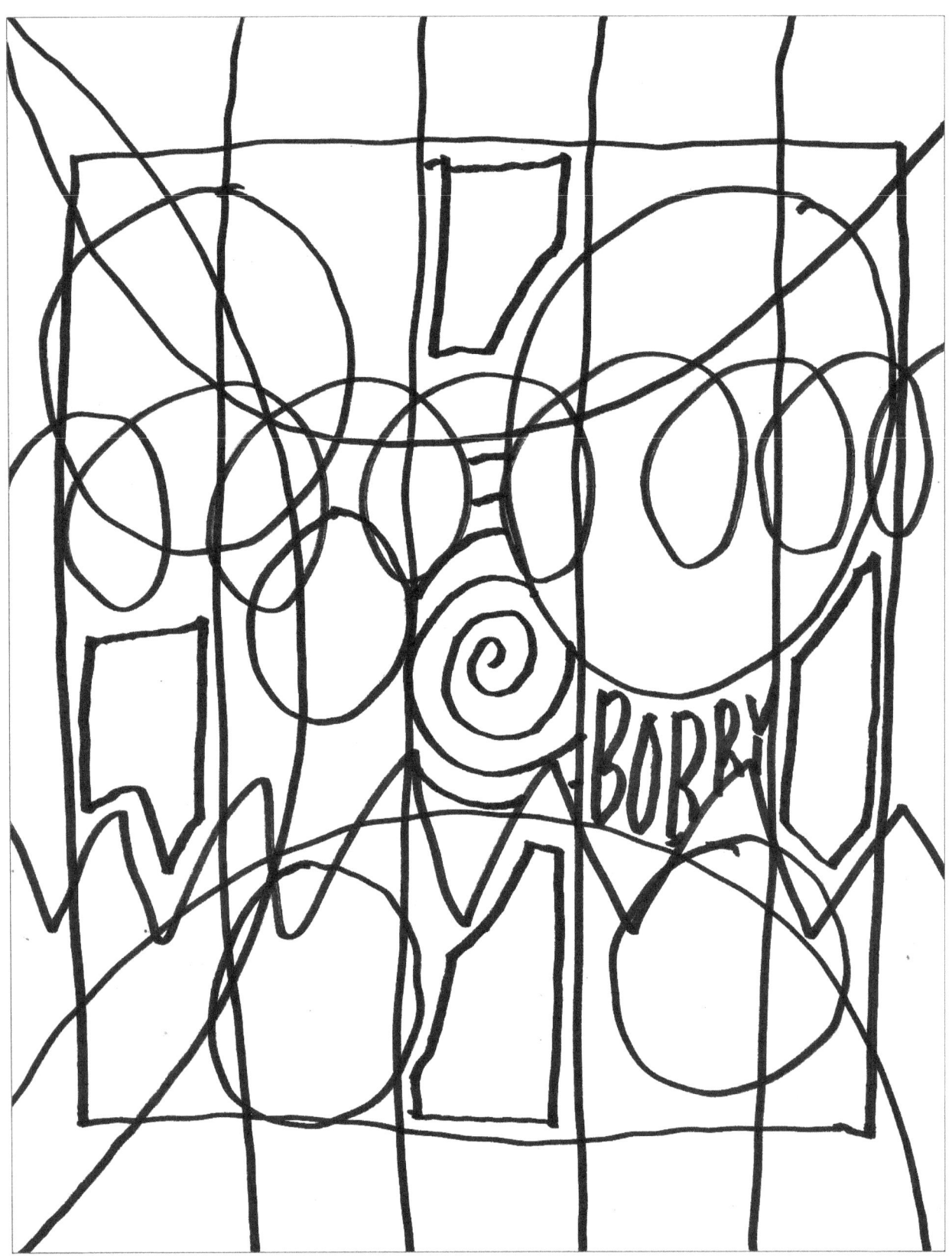

Bobby J. Jones. Black Ink Drawing #18. 2023.

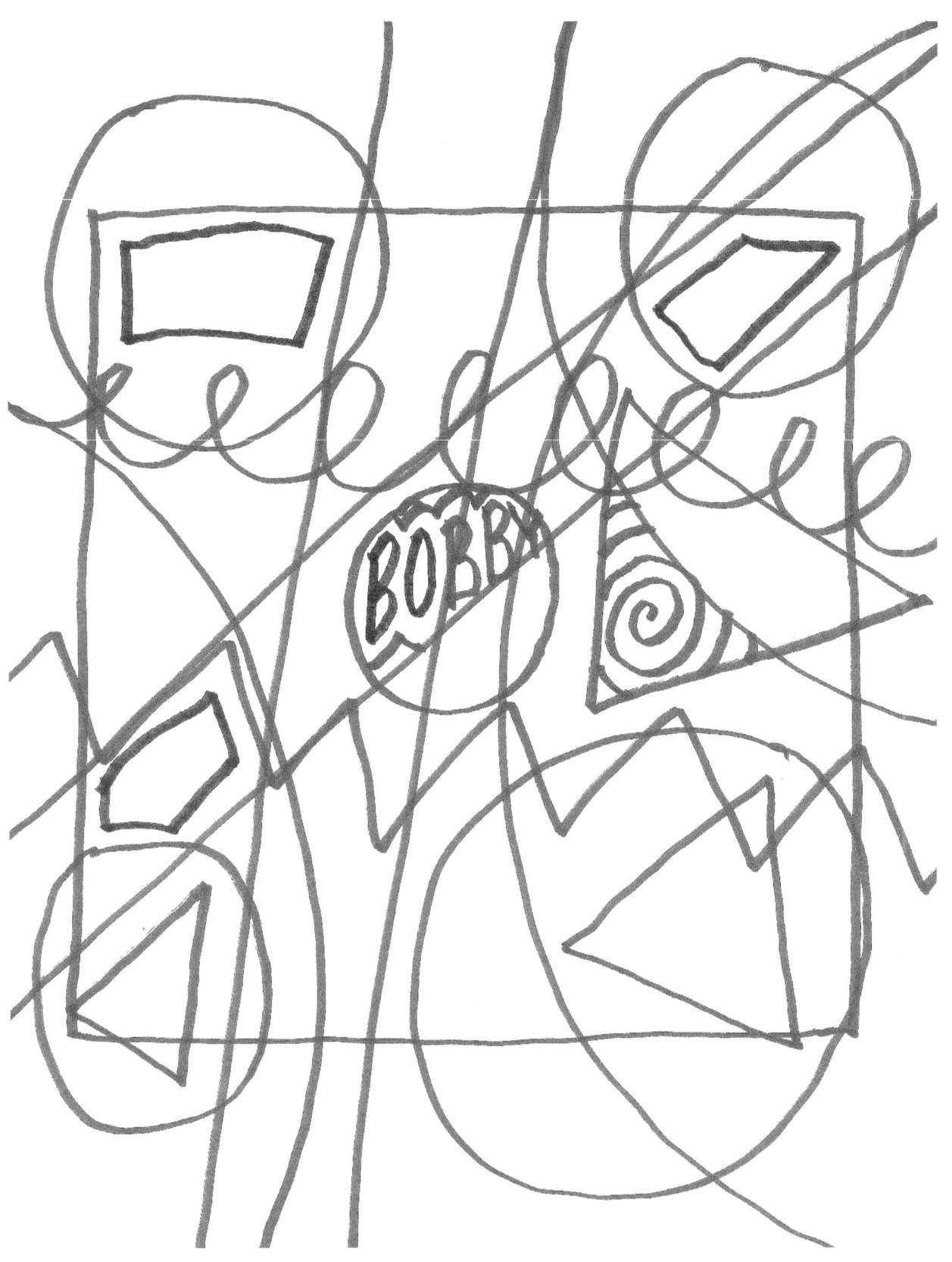

Bobby J. Jones. Black Ink Drawing #19. 2023.

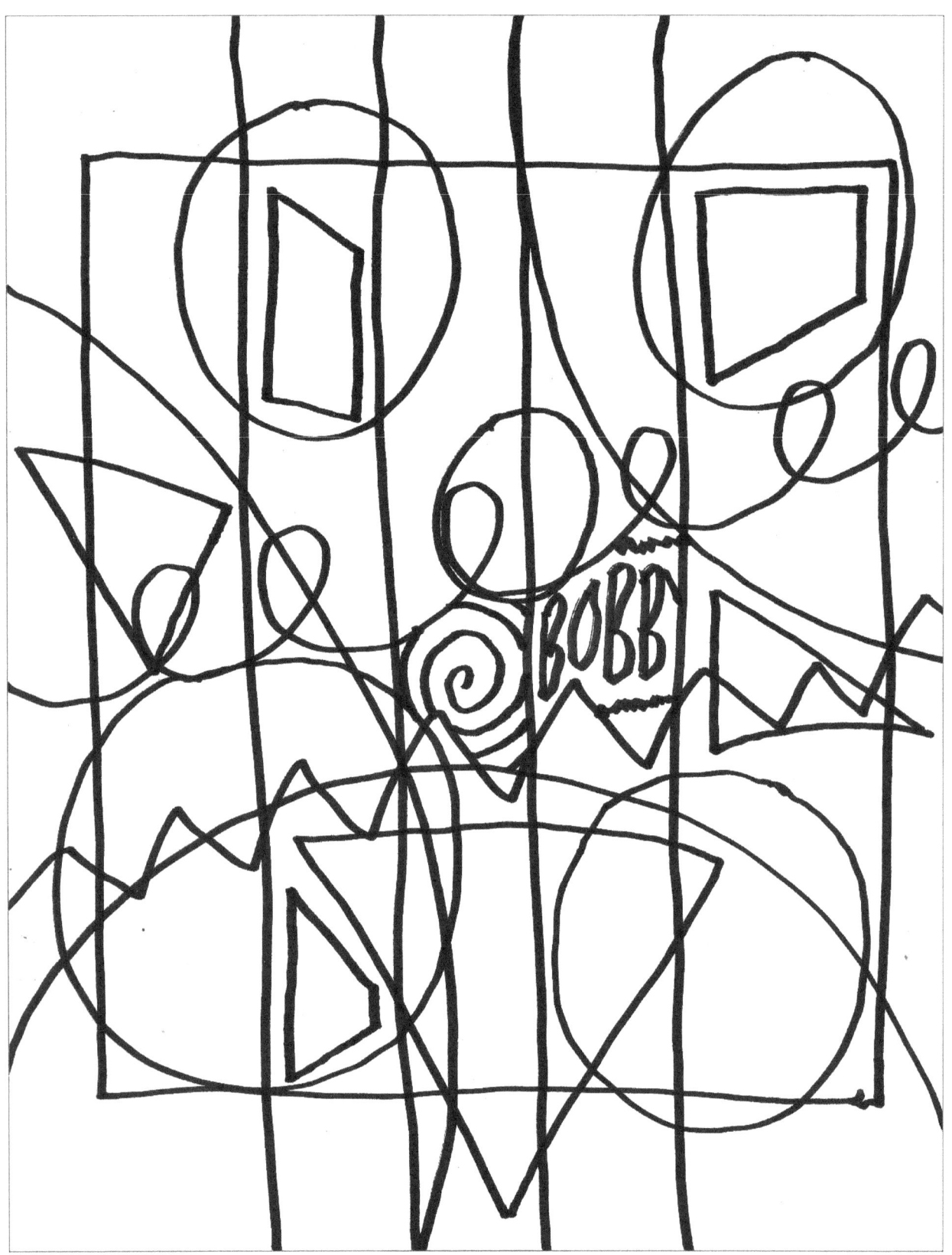

Bobby J. Jones. Black Ink Drawing #20. 2023.

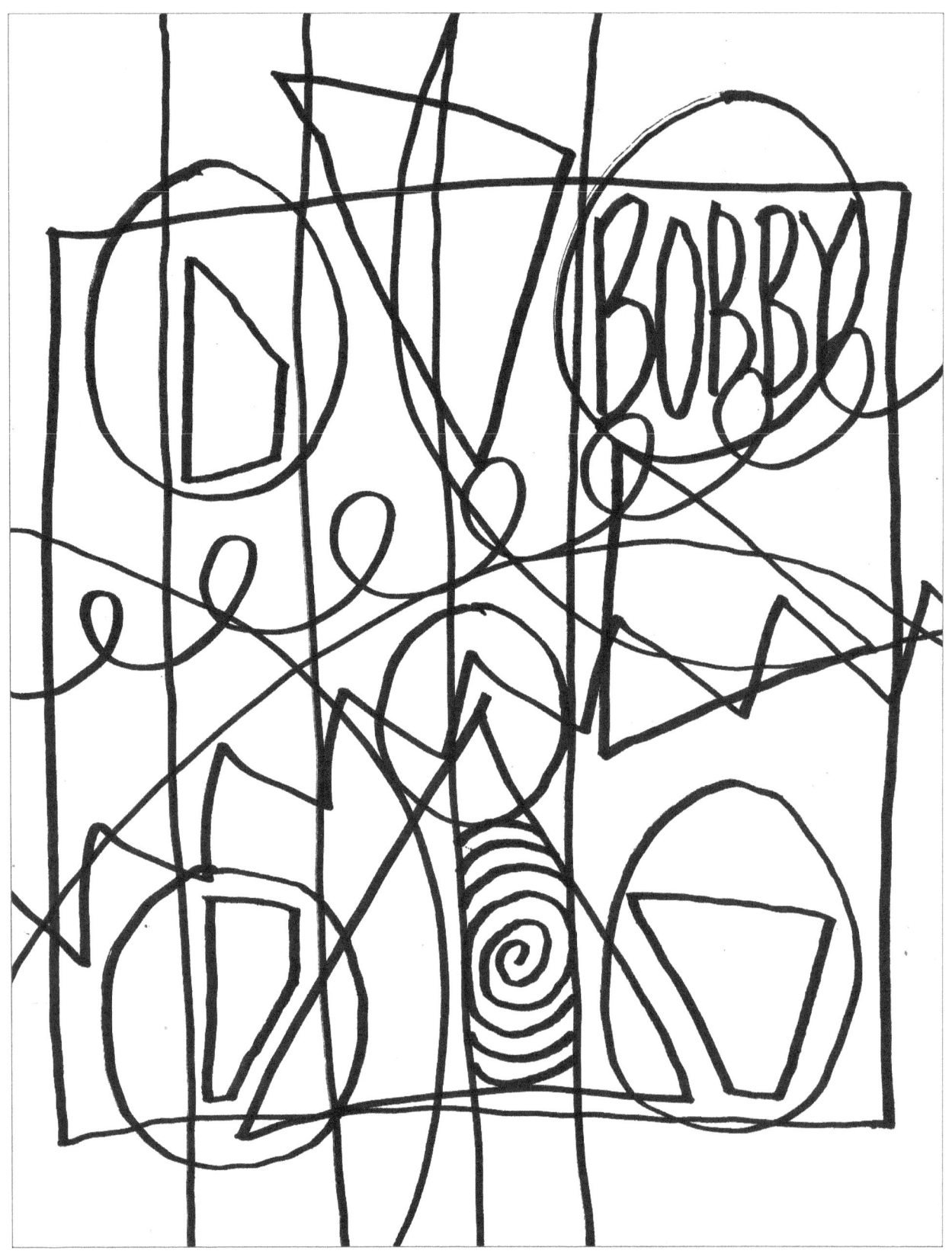

Bobby J. Jones. Black Ink Drawing #21. 2023.

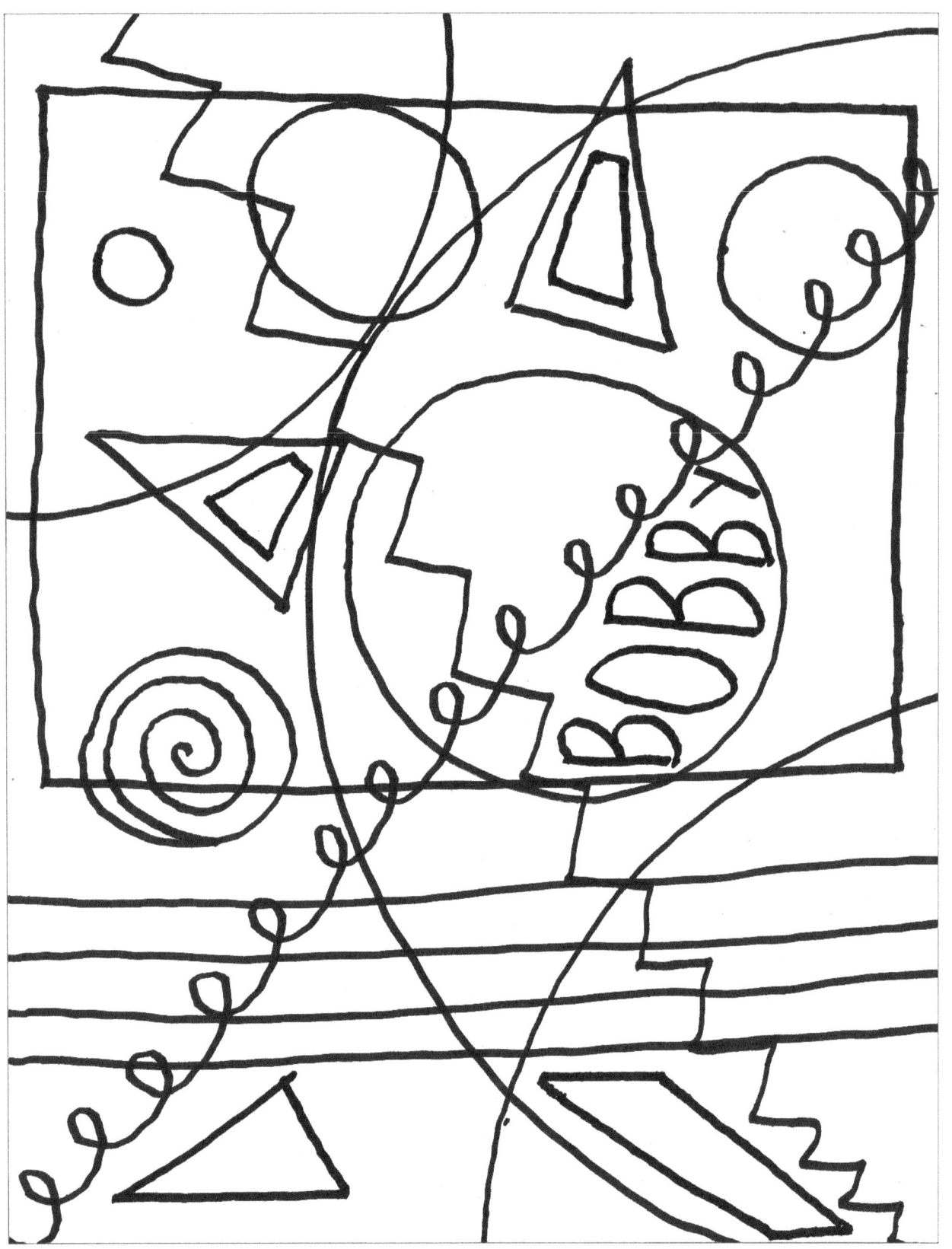

Bobby J. Jones. Black Ink Drawing #22. 2023.

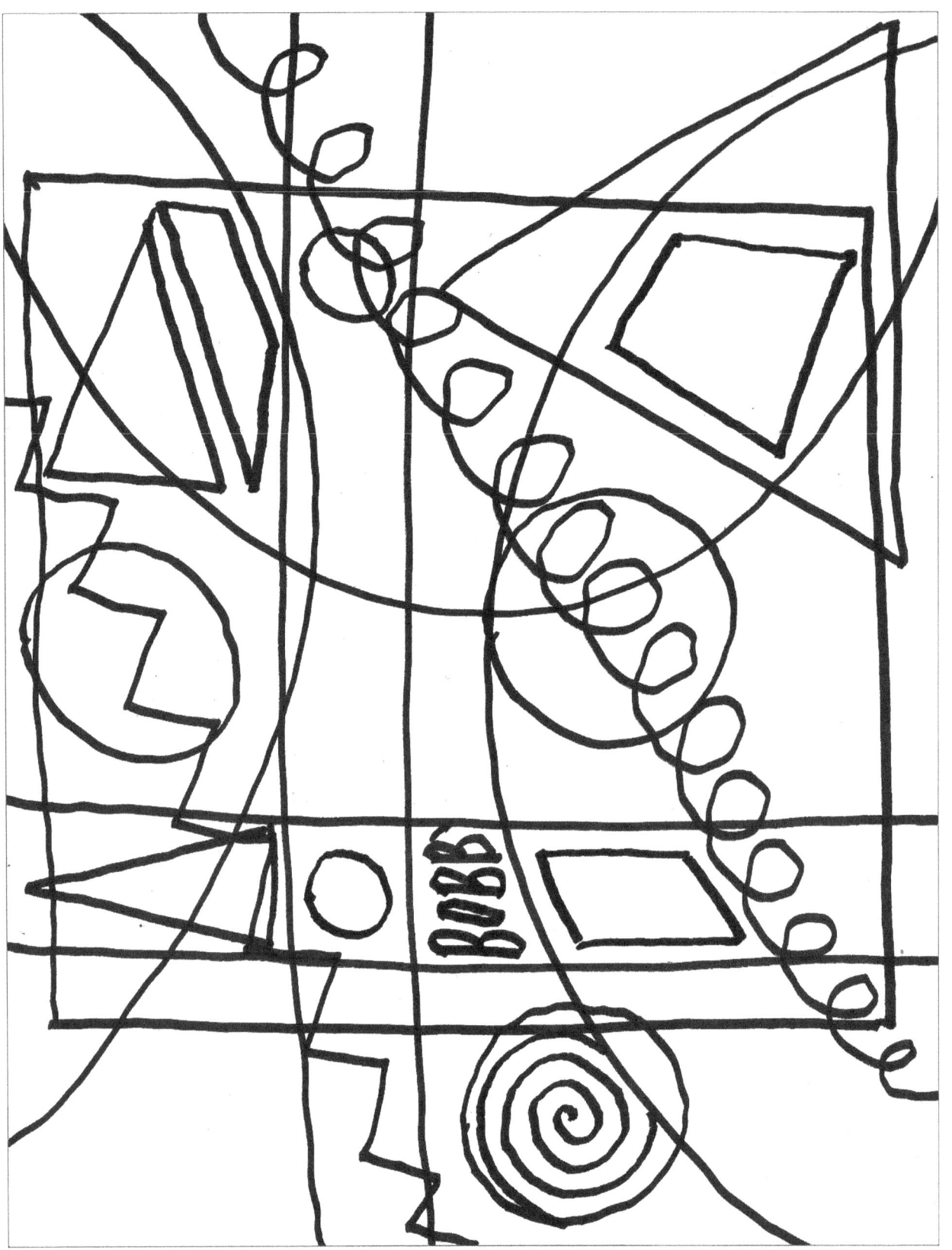

Bobby J. Jones. Black Ink Drawing #23. 2023.

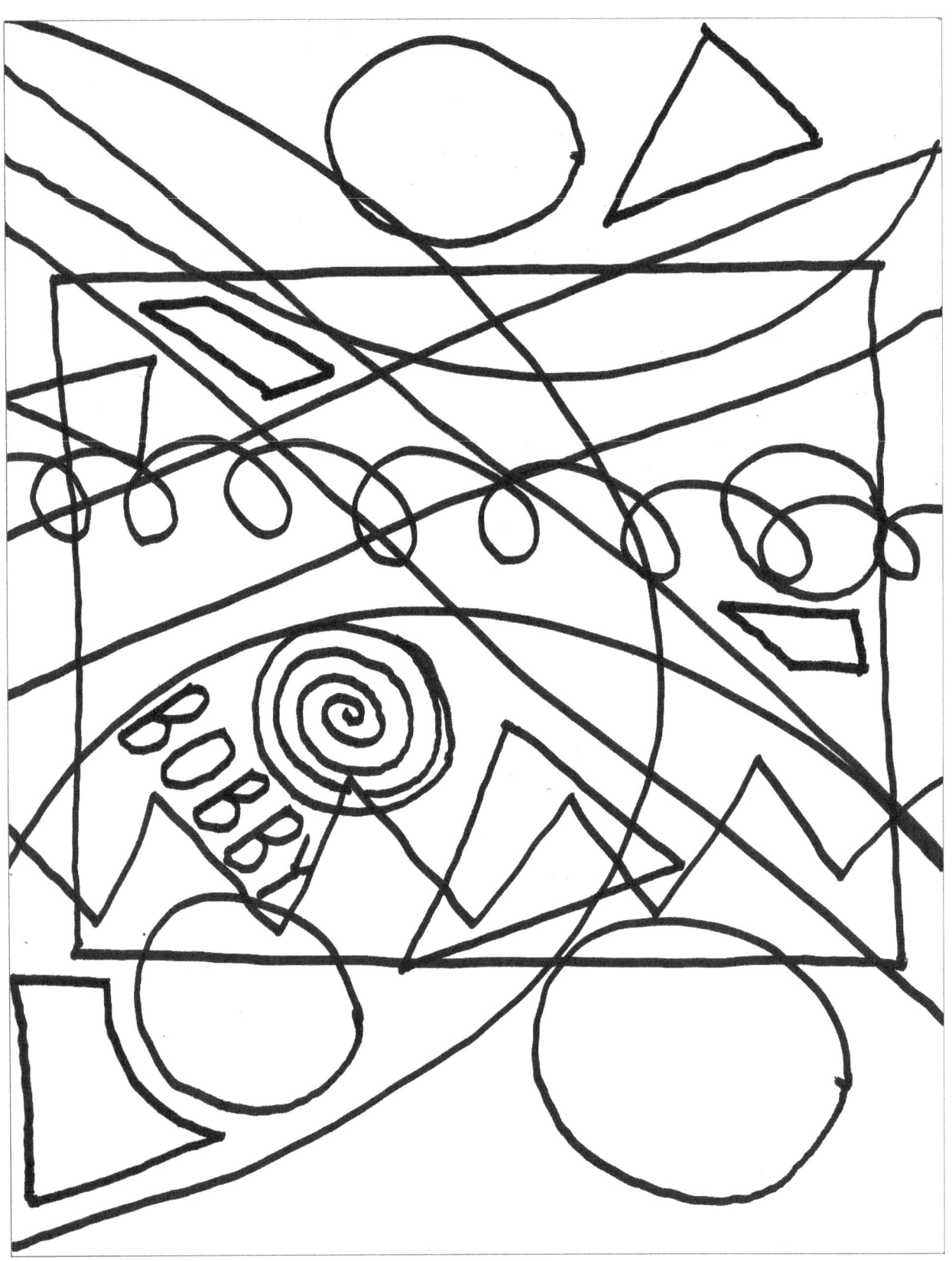

Bobby J. Jones. Black Ink Drawing #24. 2023.

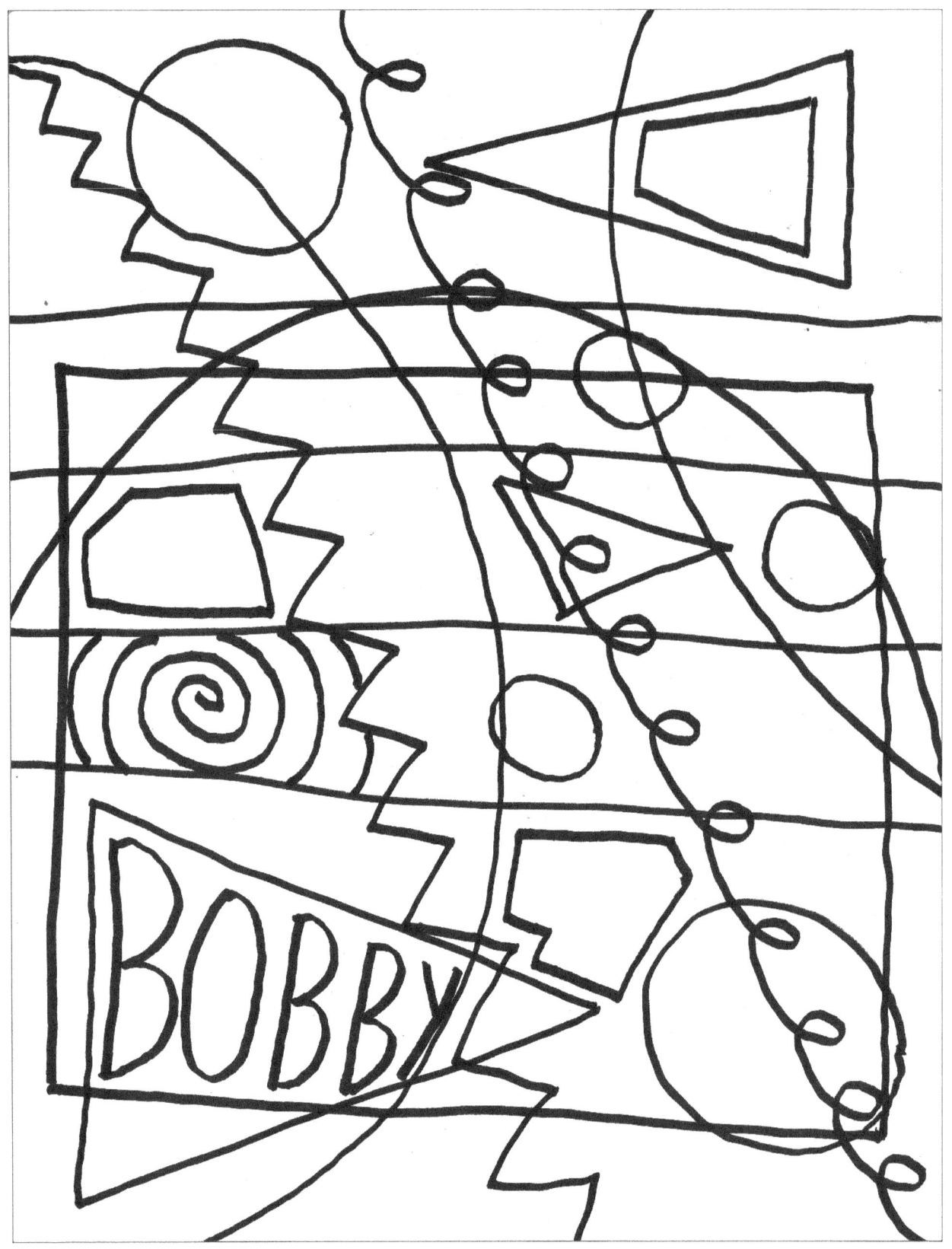

Bobby J. Jones. Black Ink Drawing #25. 2023.

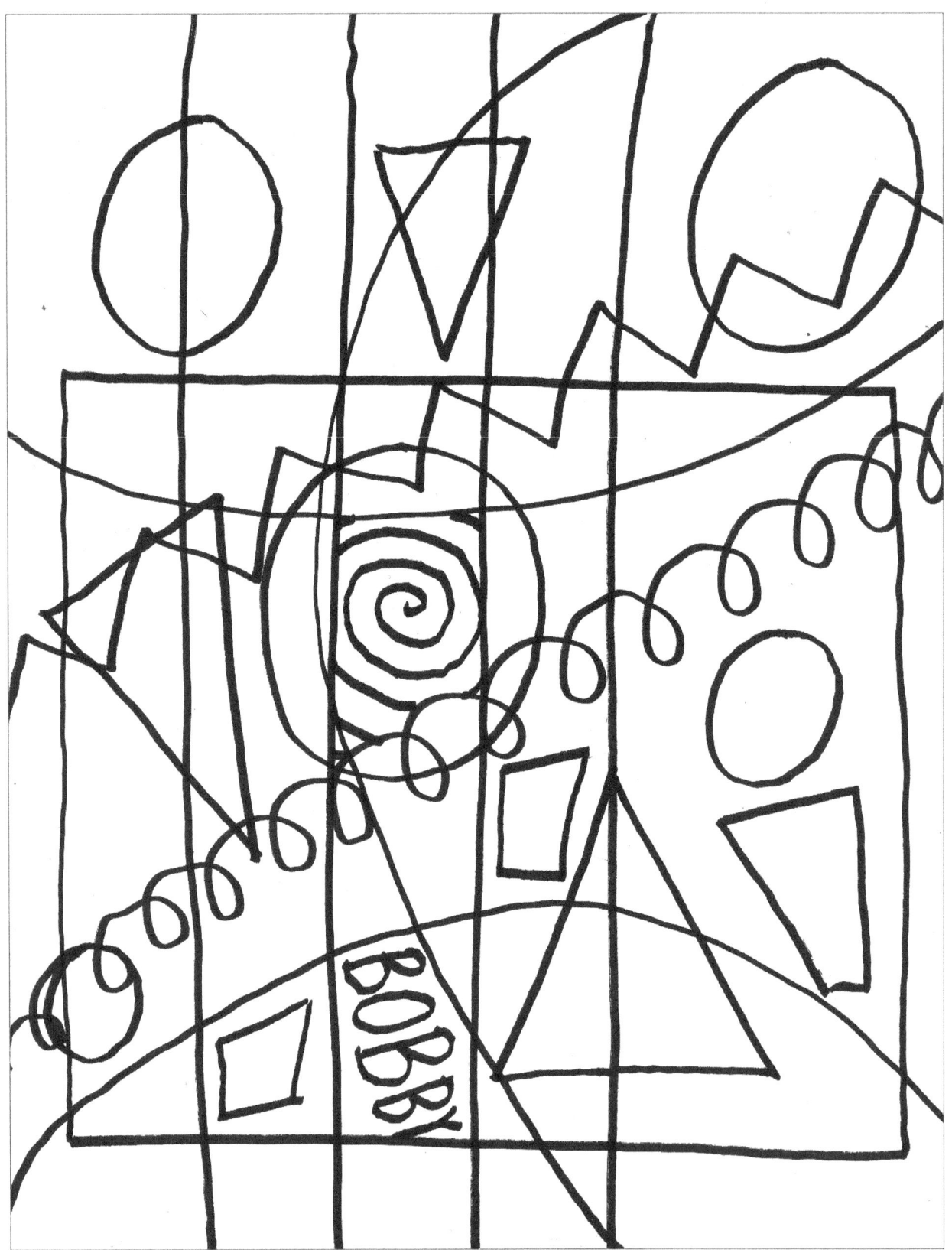

Bobby J. Jones. Black Ink Drawing #26. 2023.

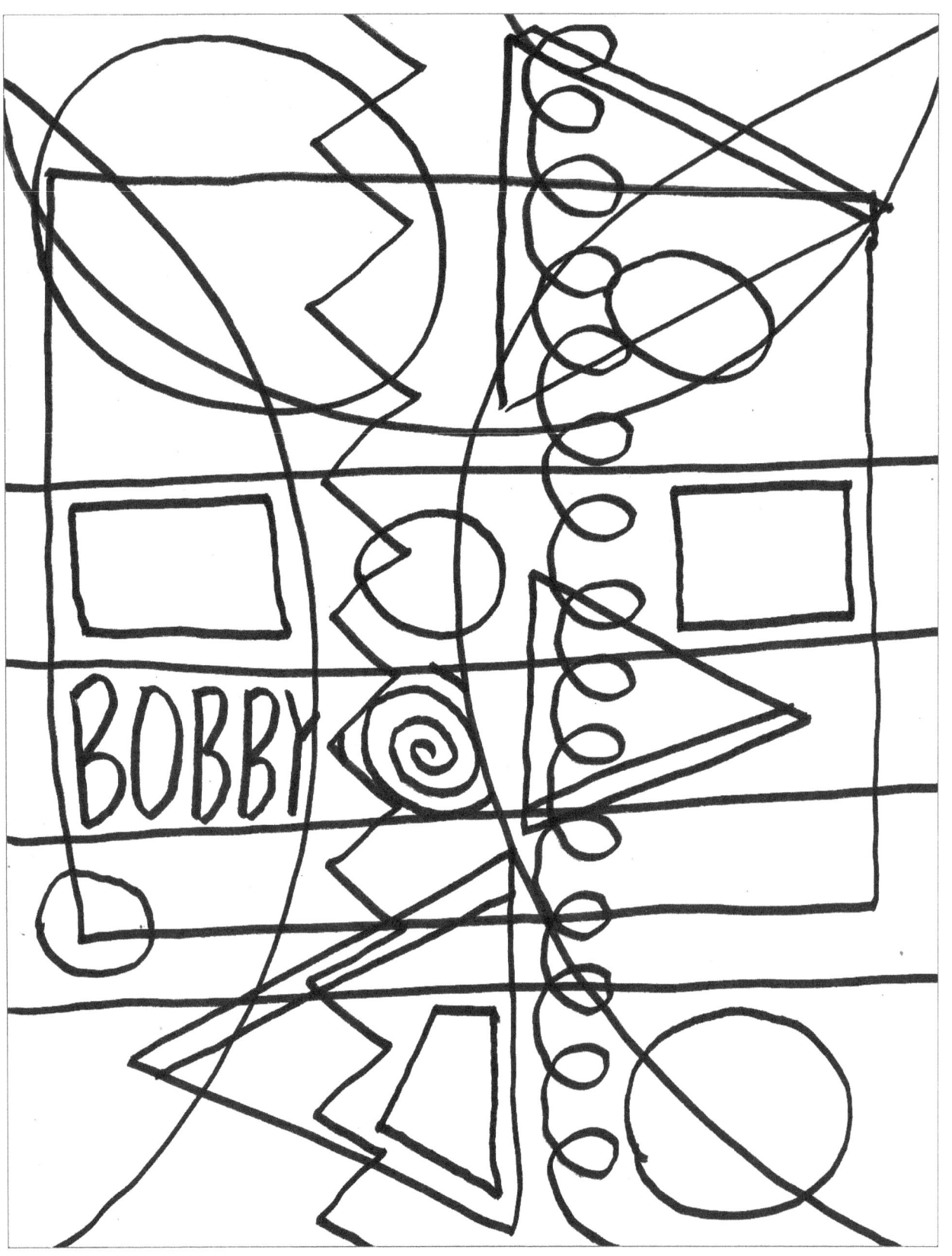

Bobby J. Jones. Black Ink Drawing #27. 2023.

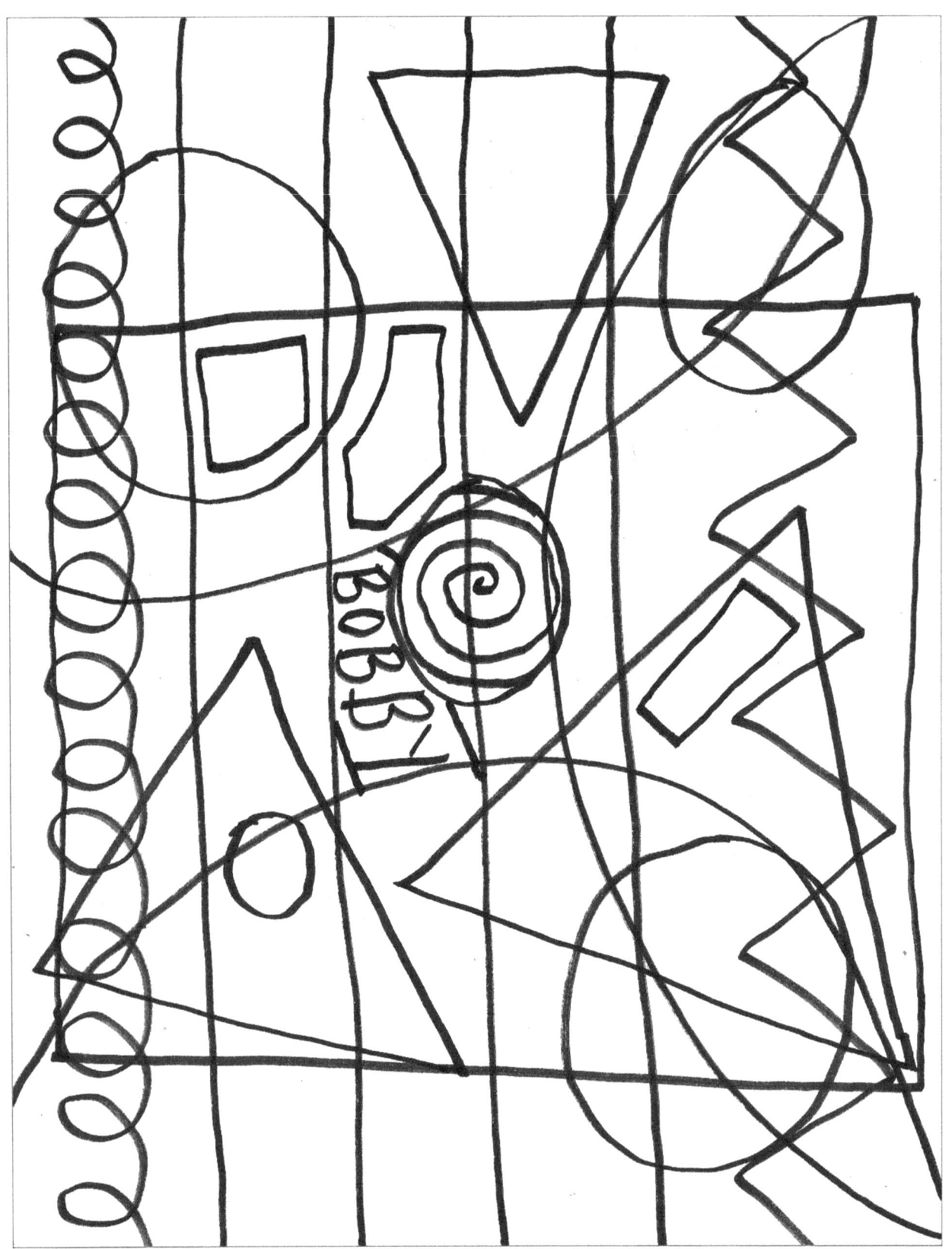

Bobby J. Jones. Black Ink Drawing #28. 2023.

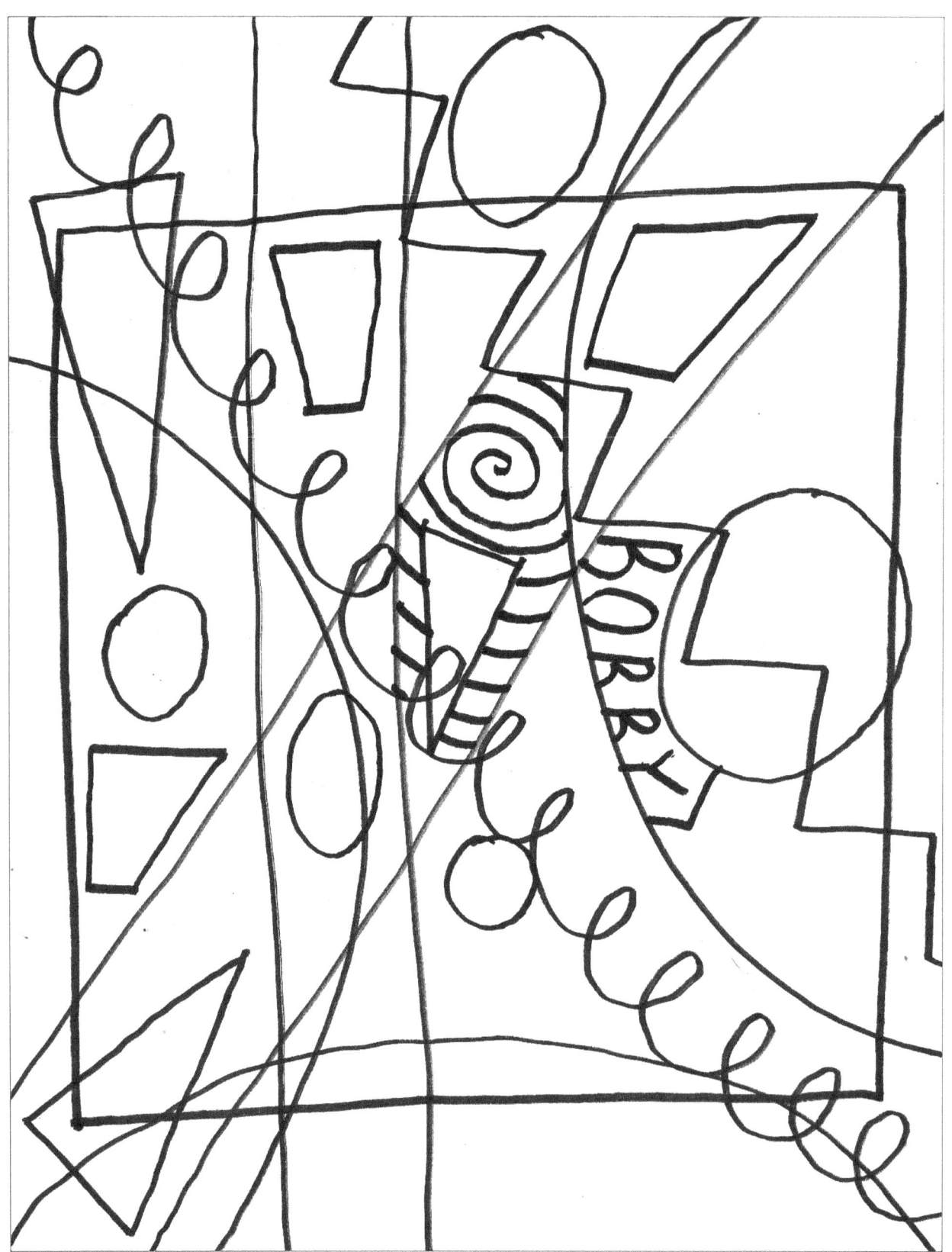

Bobby J. Jones. Black Ink Drawing #29. 2023.

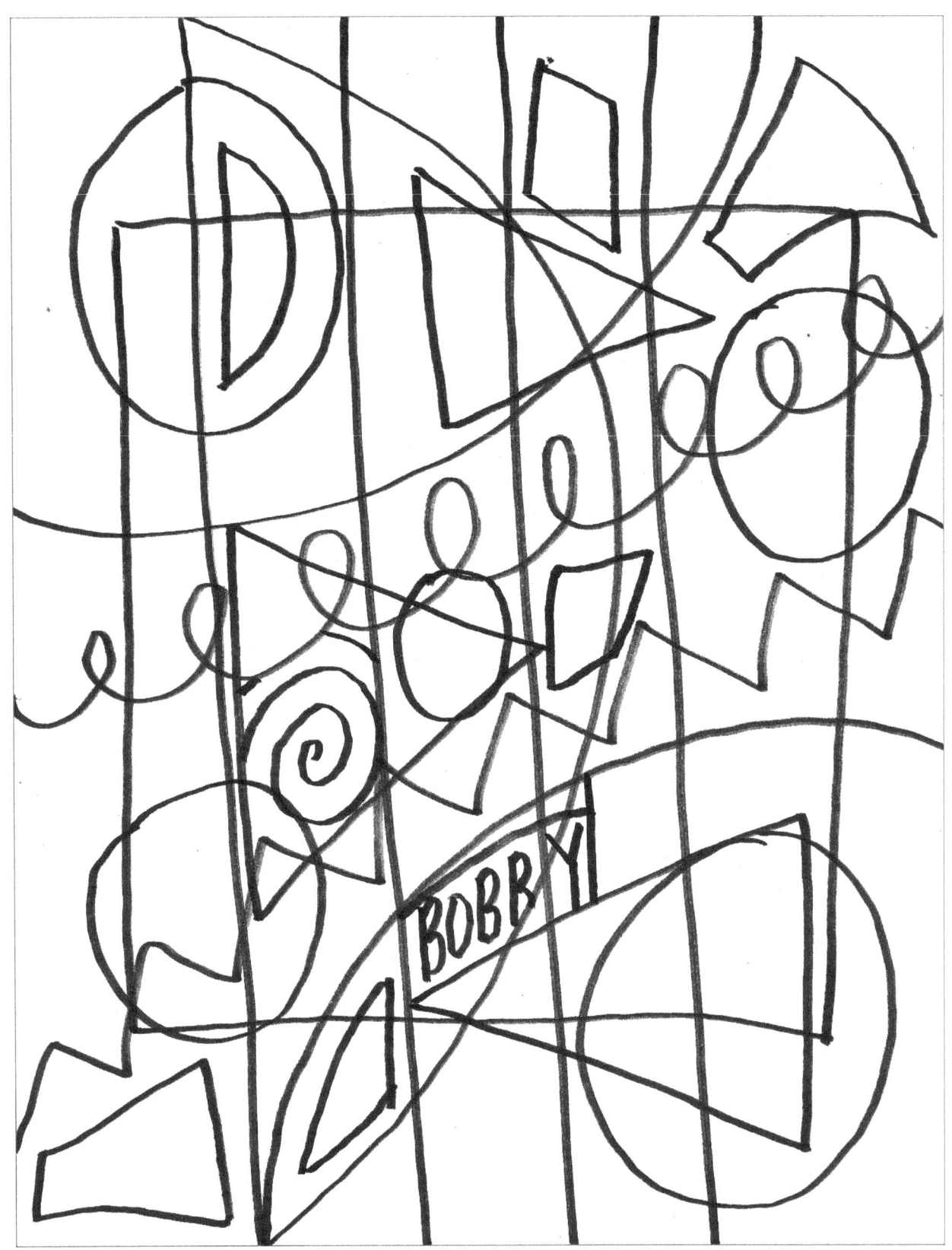

Bobby J. Jones. Black Ink Drawing #30. 2023.

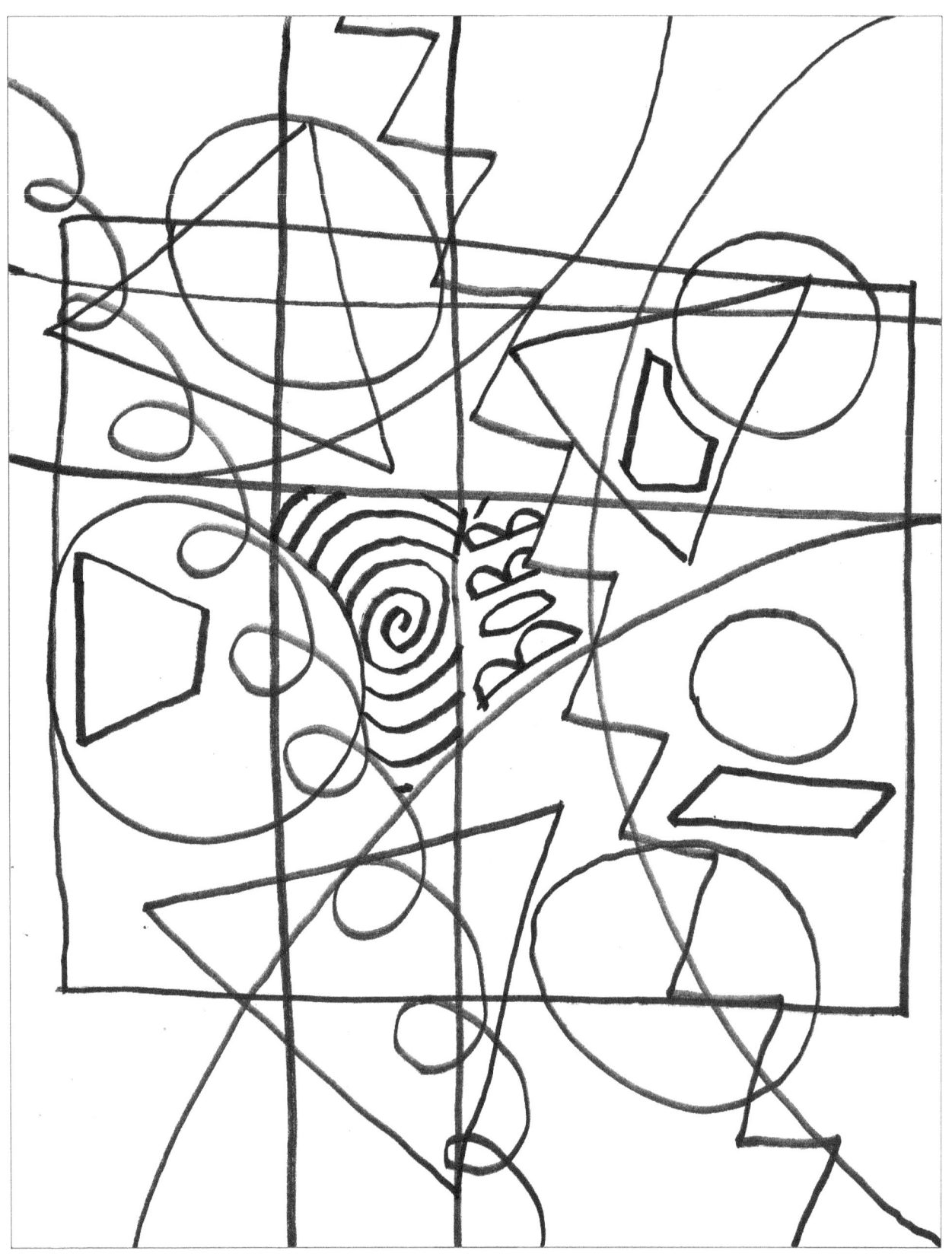

Bobby J. Jones. Black Ink Drawing #31. 2023.

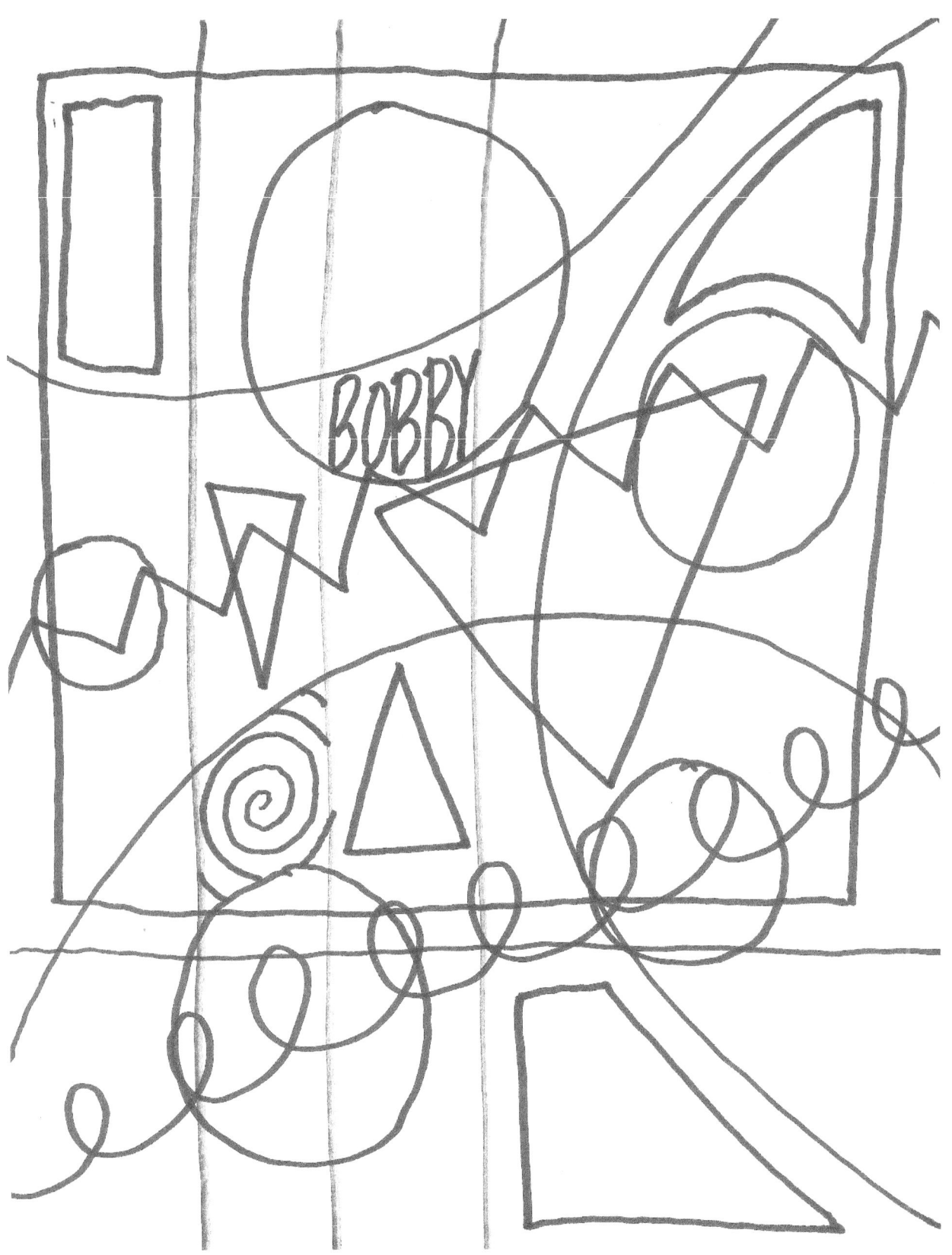

Bobby J. Jones. Black Ink Drawing #32. 2023.

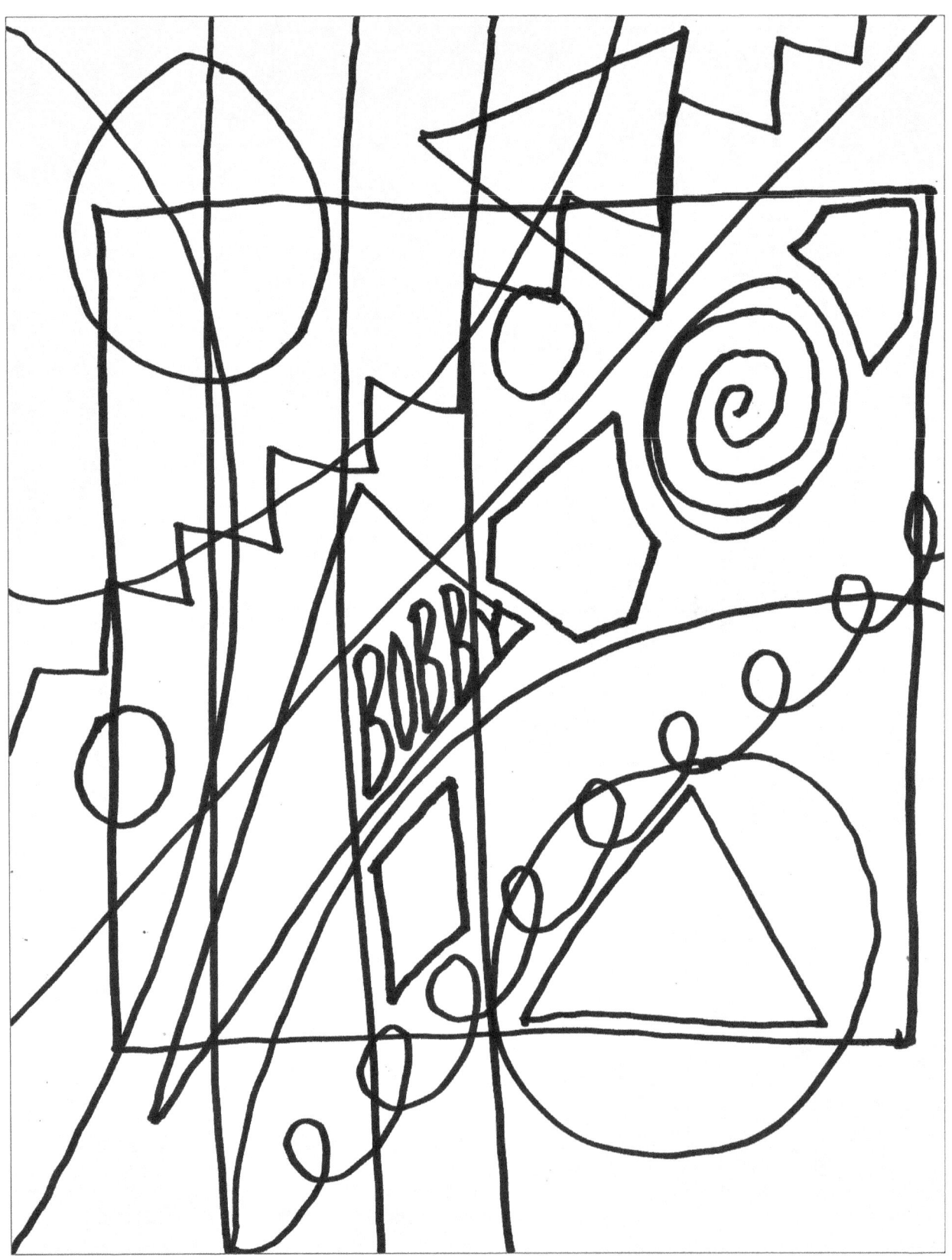

Bobby J. Jones. Black Ink Drawing #33. 2023.

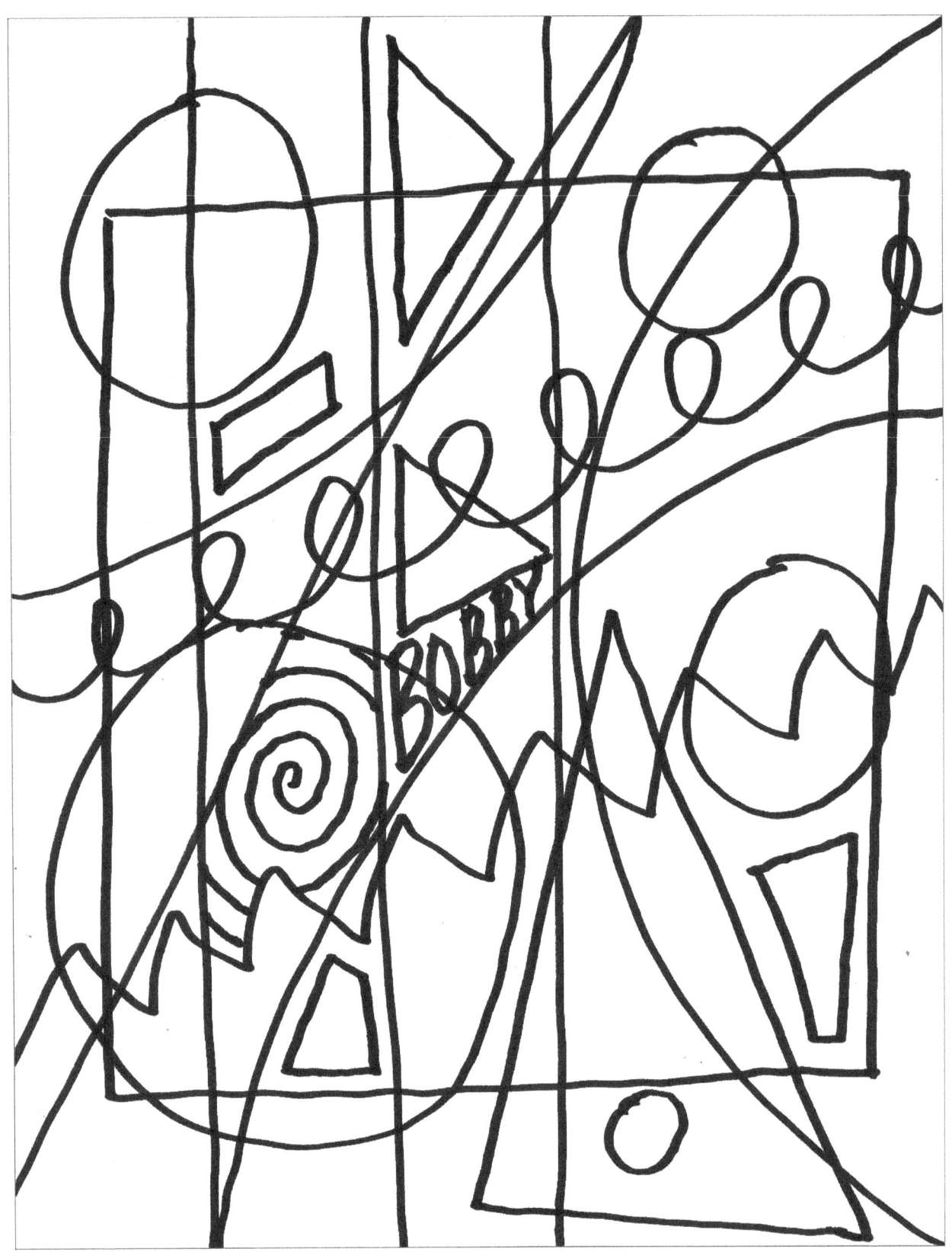

Bobby J. Jones. Black Ink Drawing #34. 2023.

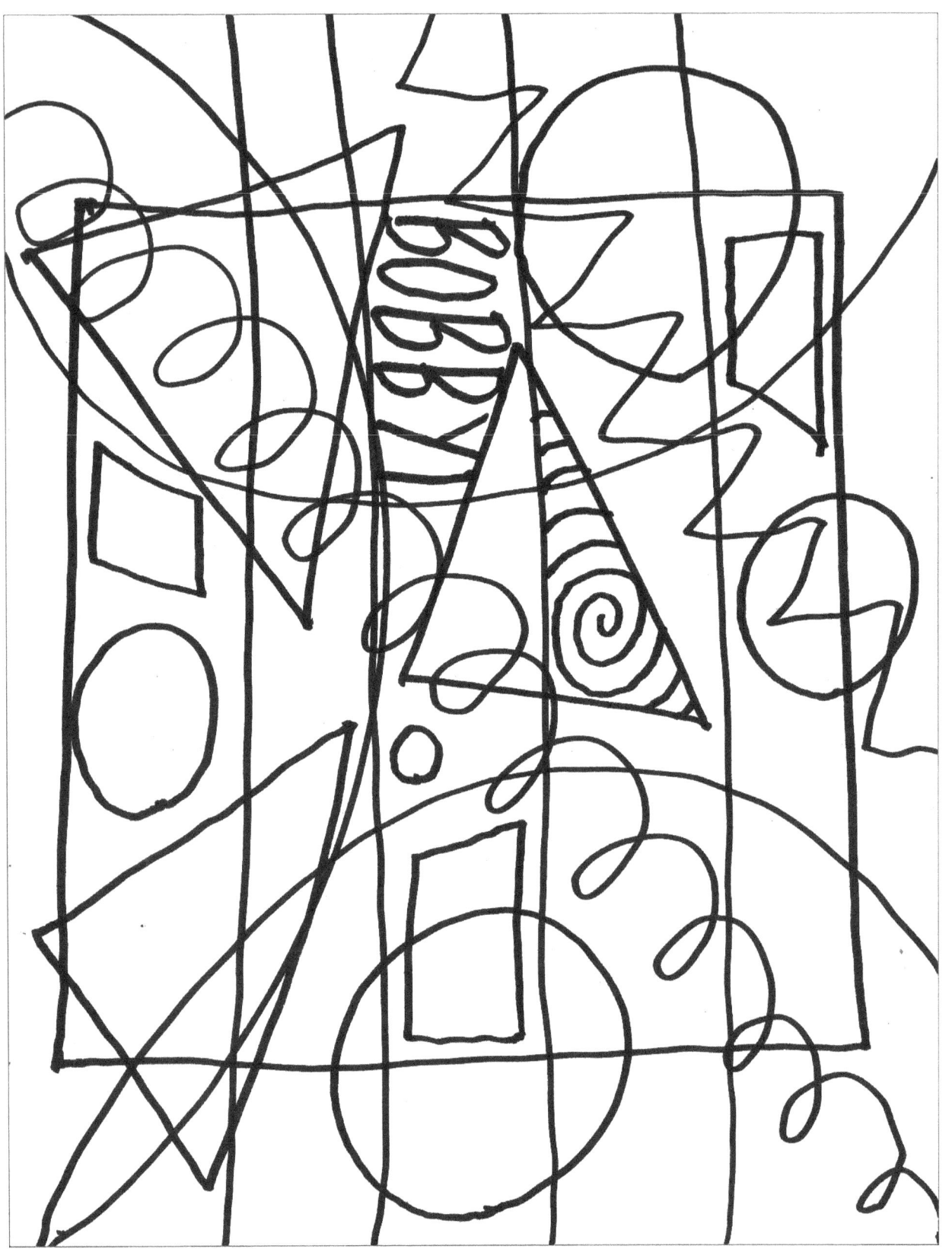

Bobby J. Jones. Black Ink Drawing #35. 2023.

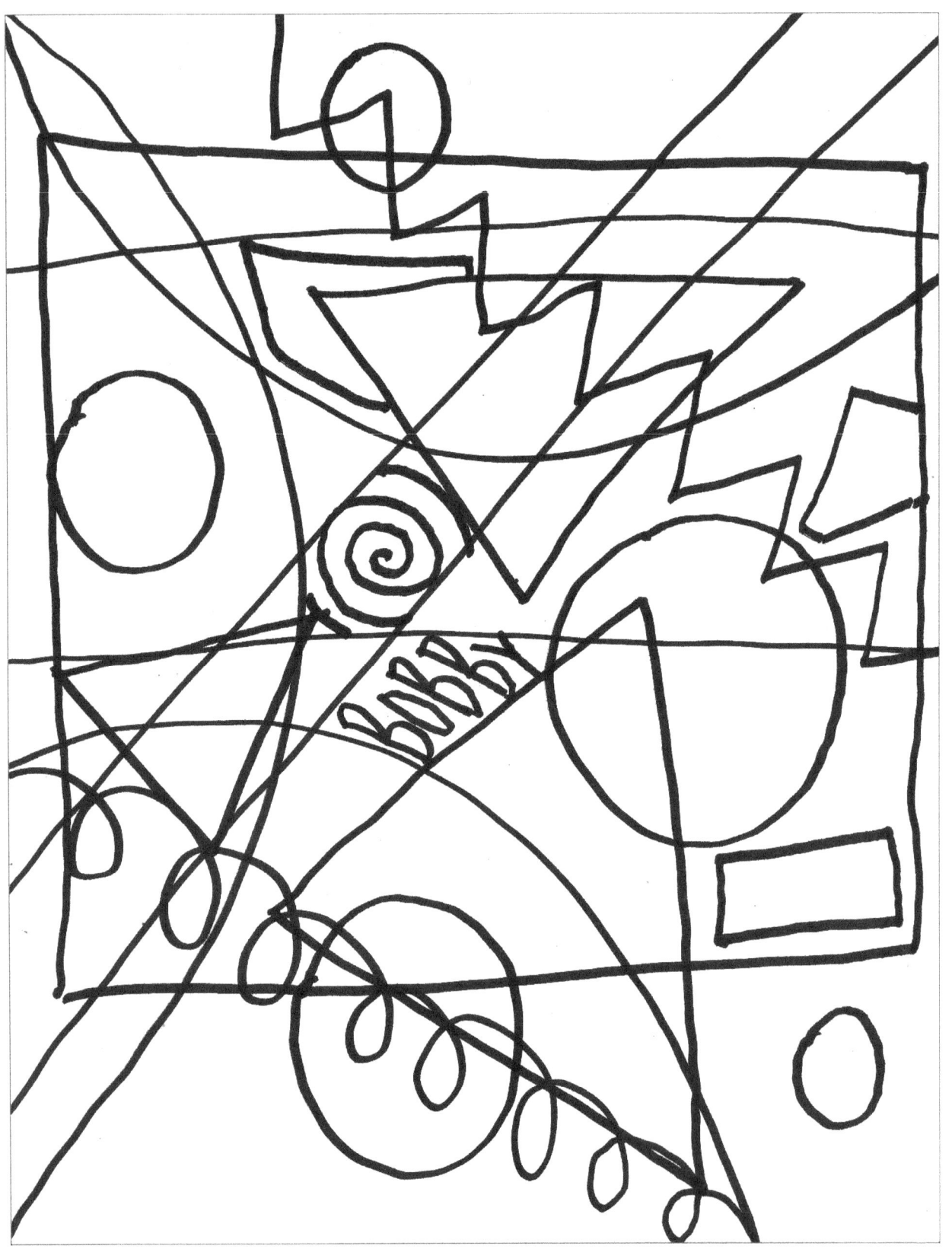

Bobby J. Jones. Black Ink Drawing #36. 2023.

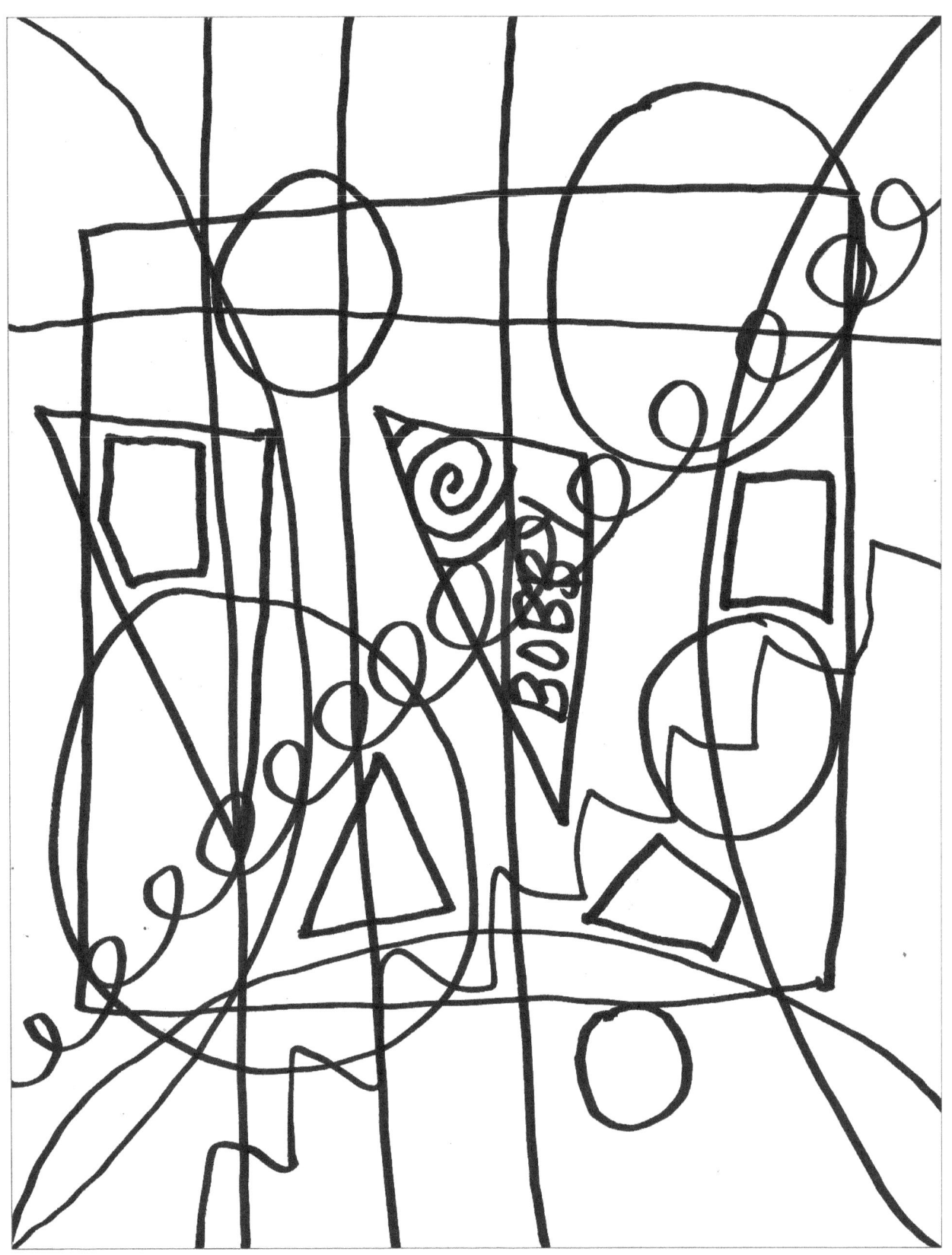

Bobby J. Jones. Black Ink Drawing #37. 2023.

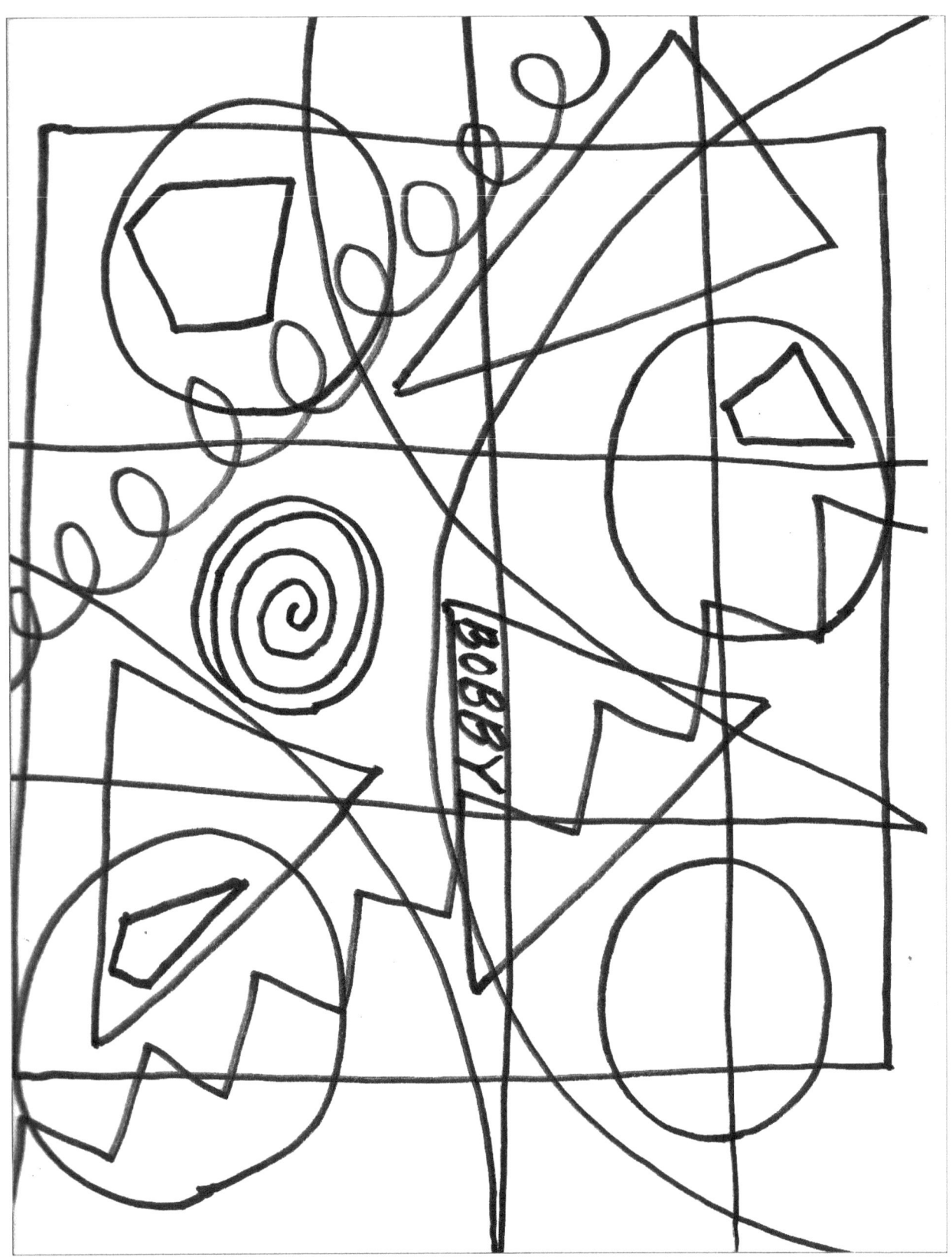

ABOUT THE AUTHOR

New Mexico Artist Bobby J. Jones was born in Lubbock, Texas at Reese Air Force Base in 1966. Bobby grew up in Fort Worth, Texas and graduated from Southwest High School in 1985. Bobby attended Texas Tech University from 1985 to 1989. He received his BFA in Art (Painting and Drawing) in 1989. Jones is a lifetime member of Alpha Phi Omega and Golden Key National Honor Society at Texas Tech University. His BFA Exhibit at Texas Tech was featured on the front page of The University Daily, March, 1989.

Bobby moved to Albuquerque, New Mexico in 1989 after graduating from his family's alma mater. He attended The University of New Mexico. This artist graduated from The University of New Mexico with a Masters in Art Education (Museum Education, Ceramics, and Photography). While Jones attended UNM, he exhibited his art in The Art Education Gallery inside Masley Hall in The College of Education.

Jones currently lives in Albuquerque, New Mexico after living in California for 12 years. He moved to The Land of Enchantment in 2009 and works for Albuquerque Public Schools. During this time, Jones continues to focus on creating his artwork. He combines his painting and drawing skills upon the surface of his paintings.

Jones' painting Brighter Days Ahead was recognized by The 2020 Taos Art Insurgency Committee and selected for Director's Choice. This painting along with his other painting Singing Out To The Skies were exhibited in The Protagonists Exhibit in The Wilder Nightingale Fine Art Gallery, July, 2020, Taos, New Mexico.

Bobby was recognized by The 2021 Luxembourg Art Prize Committee by receiving A Certificate of Merit for participating. Jones is not only a member of The Matrix Fine Art Gallery. He is selling his artwork at Southwest Treasures in Cottonwood Mall in Albuquerque, New Mexico. This New Mexico artist has also exhibited at The South Broadway Cultural Center, The Albuquerque Museum, The Anderson-Abruzzo International Balloon Museum, The Matrix Gallery, David Naylor Interior Design Showroom, The Black Wall Art Gallery, and The Tortuga Gallery. His work was featured in online nationwide and international art exhibits. He is also a member of The Biafarin Company in Ontario, Canada. He is also selling his artwork at his Art Storefronts account at www.bobbyjonesart.com.

And now, Jones has created his most current art publication, The Contemporary Black Ink Drawings of Bobby J. Jones Coloring Book. He has other coloring books and future art projects. They involve creating art publications of his artwork and his photographs.

www.ingramcontent.com/pod-product-compliance
Lightning Source LLC
Chambersburg PA
CBHW081452220526
45466CB00008B/2602